SECURITIES
S E R V

REPORTS & ACCOUNTS DEMYSTIFIED

PROFESSIONALISM | INTEGRITY | EXCELLENCE

REPORTS & ACCOUNTS DEMYSTIFIED

EDDIE HILL

First printed in Great Britain 2003 by
Securities Institute (Services) Limited
Centurion House, 24 Monument Street
London EC3R 8AQ, England.

Written by Eddie Hill

ISBN: 1 84307 063 4
First edition printed May 2003

Printed and bound in Great Britain by
Antony Rowe Limited, Chippenham, Wiltshire

Contents

PREFACE

This book attempts to describe and analyse the contents and structure of audited public company reports and accounts, what they mean and how potential investors or lenders should view and interpret them.

In doing so, it also explains the key determinants of the investment or lending decisions based on this analysis, the impact of these decisions on financial structures and performance, and why apparently profitable companies can still go bankrupt.

It is aimed not at accountants, but at finance professionals who need to have a working knowledge of these documents. It accordingly takes a non-technical approach in an attempt to make it more accessible, but acknowledges that due to the complexity of the subject matter and the issues involved, a certain level of technicality is unavoidable.

To put the current state of company reporting into context, the introduction includes a brief history of UK and international accounting, a review of the statutory and regulatory environment and a summary of the key elements of the accounts.

It then goes into more detail on these elements, focusing on the issues involved, the import of the accounting standards, the reasons for the methodologies adopted, and the range of possible outcomes, including those that could be regarded as unsatisfactory. Although this part of the book may come across as being highly critical of the standards and their application, it should be recognised that, although not perfect, they are a very good start and further improvement is continuous.

The above Chapters are then brought into context, with a review of the analytical methodologies applied and the uses to which the accounts are put, acknowledging the weaknesses of the base information provided.

The accounts themselves are hybrid documents, serving the dual purposes of providing shareholders with the legally required level of financial information and providing company management with the opportunity to highlight good performance or explain poor performance, all with the primary agenda of persuading people to buy or to retain the shares, and thus keep the company independent.

Having looked at how the accounts may be interpreted, we then look briefly at management accounting and budgeting, how companies manage financial risk, the main drivers of how they raise finance and the types of finance commonly used.

The book also includes a review of the main differences between UK and international accounting standards, the current moves to codify then harmonise these standards and the potential impact on UK companies of this process.

It concludes with a summary of the current state of the key areas of legislation and regulation (accounting standards, audit and corporate governance) and current "hot" issues that are taxing the profession.

Company law and regulation, and the accounting standards behind them, are subject to continuous change, and it is likely that the position with regard to a number of issues will have changed between the final draft and the publication of this book.

Indeed, during the writing of this Preface, the review of governance conducted by Derek Higgs, referred to in the text, has produced its report, along with a first draft of a proposed new Code of Corporate Governance. The report and the draft code have provoked a storm of controversy and some widely divergent views, depending on which side of the fence the holder is sitting, and doubtless a long period of consultation and drafting will commence.

Other very problematic factors in the corporate environment during the production of this book, albeit affecting the tone rather than the content of this book, were the dramatic collapse in the value of many companies in the dot.com sector and the series of catastrophic frauds, highly questionable accounting practices and corporate collapses that occurred during 2001/2.

These events had an enormous concomitant knock-on effect on global stock markets, and were accompanied by the prosecution and subsequent disappearance of Arthur Andersen, once the world's largest audit firm.

Although I expressed the view in the text that accounting standards and regulation in themselves were not necessarily at fault, but that some of the people applying and auditing them were misguided at best, it was difficult to ignore the huge backlash of scorn, cynicism and mistrust that resulted from the events of 2001/2. In the light of these events, it would be difficult for anybody to mount a robust defence of the accounting profession, leave alone someone who is not only not an accountant, but is a cynical ex-banker and an unhappy pension and endowment policy-holder.

The best I could do was to try to remain objective, so I hope that the resultant tone of the book is as balanced as it could be under the circumstances.

I should like to close by saying that, during my career, I have worked either closely with or among accountants since 1980, and can happily state that, in the main, they are a highly intelligent, hard-working and fun bunch of people, and that contrary to popular belief, neither they nor the profession are boring. I am happy to count a number of them amongst my best friends.

Although the practice of their profession is not perfect, it has improved considerably in recent years and will continue to do so. However, the undoubted conclusion is that it could do better.

ABOUT THE AUTHOR

Eddie Hill is a treasury and corporate banking expert, with 30 years experience in the City, including 8 years in clearing banking, 13 years in senior corporate treasury roles and 10 years in corporate finance consulting with a Top 10 accounting firm. His employers have included NatWest Bank Plc, Unigate Plc, Warner Communications, EMI, Arthur Andersen and the BBC.

He is an honours graduate in Economics, was elected a Member of the Association of Corporate Treasurers in 1986 and became a Freeman of the City of London in 1995.

He is currently working as a freelance writer and corporate finance consultant, and has a number of writing projects in hand, including $1^1/_2$ novels and a feature film script.

His passions & interests include the media, some sports, contemporary English literature, geopolitics, current affairs and business finance.

ACKNOWLEDGEMENTS

I am indebted to a number of people in the writing of this book.

I would like to thank my good friend Penny Griffiths for my introduction to Debra Wilson of the Securities Institute, and Debra herself for her enthusiasm for the project and her diligence in chasing the early drafts.

I should also like to thank Tim Bennett for his help with the structure and content of the book, and Tim Donovan and Kalbinder Dhillon for their incredible thoroughness and professionalism during the later drafting and proofreading stages, which I cannot think would have been an easy or particularly enjoyable task.

I should also like to thank my good friends Dean Brown and Paul Rathbone for dealing thoroughly, professionally and patiently with my questions, and for providing much entertainment with their subsequent "off the record" personal views and analysis.

Finally, I should like to thank my partner Nicola Chandler for her support and indulgence, and my children, Nikki, Alexander and Olivia for providing me with the fiscal incentive to get it finished.

Although as much care as possible has gone into the writing and production of this book, it will almost undoubtedly contain some errors, omissions or anachronisms at the time of publication. For these, I apologise.

1

INTRODUCTION

1. Background

At first sight, the most striking things about company reports and accounts (Accounts) are the quality of finish, the eye-catching pictorial content and the upbeat tone and bullish narrative from the chairman, the chief executive and the finance director. It sometimes seems that the dry financial information is tucked away at the back, almost as an afterthought.

This is because the accounts are the key source of information about a company, which is aimed at and sent to existing and potential new shareholders. They must, therefore, create a positive impression, leaving the shareholders in no doubt that their investment is safe in the hands of the company's management.

To achieve this, the accounts must perform the dual role of a marketing/PR document and a factual report that represents a true and fair view of the financial position of the company. This is quite a difficult task to achieve and, whilst most companies make a reasonably good job of the marketing aspects of the accounts, they are typically less successful in communicating clearly their true financial position.

As a result, most laymen are baffled by financial reporting, and most of their attempts to glean the answers to what are relatively simple questions are frustrated.

For example, there are no fewer than nine profit subtotals in the BOC profit & loss Account shown in Chapter 2, Section 1.1.3. Which one is significant for the shareholders and which are significant for the company? The balance sheet may show lower net assets than for the previous year, but the share price may be higher. A company may be generating operating profits but absorbing cash. What is the shareholder to make of these apparent contradictions?

The answer lies in the accounting rules which govern the figures that appear in the accounts. There are dozens of highly complex accounting and financial reporting standards in place, written and practised by countless intelligent and highly-trained professionals. Despite, or perhaps because of this, the results of their efforts are difficult to understand and are occasionally proven by subsequent events to have concealed more than they revealed. How does this happen?

Simplistically, in book-keeping terms, if a company manages to sell something for more than its cost of production, the company has made a profit on that transaction. If it sells it for less, it has made a loss. If it carries out more profitable transactions than loss-making transactions, then theoretically, at the end of its financial year, it should have more cash than at the end of the previous year.

Accounting, as distinct from book-keeping, attempts to establish exactly what it has cost to produce a sale, the correct value of assets and liabilities, and to recognise the timing differences between receipts and payments.

Unless the cost of absolutely everything utilised in producing a sale has been accurately accounted for, it is by no means certain that the sale was profitable. Assets nearing the end of their useful life will need replacing, and cash will be required to replace them. Stocks and finished goods may have been sitting in the warehouse for a long time and may not be worth the sum paid for them. There may have been an economic downturn, which potentially could cause increased bad debts or falling property values.

These factors become even more important when companies are widely owned by a disparate group of shareholders. In addition to economic and business circumstances and decisions affecting the value of the shares, factors such as strong internal audit and financial controls, and effective corporate governance (including checks and balances at board level) are very important to a company's financial health.

The current accounting, auditing and corporate governance regimes are intended to provide a common framework for tracking transaction flows through a business, for valuing assets and liabilities, and for producing coherent statements of the activity and valuations at the end of each accounting period.

Consensus around this common framework has proven difficult to achieve and the increasing complexity of business and finance have often left standard-setting and regulation in their wake.

Each new complication and each company failure that highlights a loophole in the rules require fresh analysis of the problems raised. When agreement on the precise nature of a problem is reached, discussion and consultation on potential solutions is required. Once the solution is agreed, formulation and drafting of new rules is necessary. This is extremely time-consuming, and each solution tends to create further anomalies and loopholes.

This explains why there is now a plethora of lengthy and complex accounting standards and why there is so much variety in their interpretation. In their turn, these factors perhaps explain why companies can fail despite apparently having good profits and solid-looking accounts.

The main objectives of this book are to:

- describe clearly and succinctly how and why reports and accounts are constructed, what they mean and how they may be analysed or interpreted by potential investors or lenders;

- explain the main determinants of investment or lending decisions, and the impact of the financial structure of the company (and implicitly the availability and cost of finance) on its operation and key performance ratios; and
- explain the key differences between accounting profit and cash, and why apparently profitable companies can go bankrupt.

It is not intended for accountants, but for finance professionals who need to understand the content, structure and import of a company's accounts. It does not require any prior knowledge or expertise on the part of the reader, and it attempts to facilitate the interpretation of accounts, without going into great length about the accounting processes behind them.

In doing this, it focuses on practical matters, mentioning the relevant regulatory regime and current accounting and listing rules where appropriate. It is illustrated by examples from selected public company reports and accounts.

2. A Brief History of UK and International Accounting

The search for a common business accounting framework began more than five hundred years ago. An Italian monk named Paccioli set out the basics of business accounting as an Appendix to a book on algebra. Paccioli reasoned that a set of business accounts was really only an equation by another name, and that assets and liabilities would always be equal by definition.

Whilst this worked for a simple statement of assets and liabilities, once an entity began trading, Paccioli had to decide how sales income and purchase expenditure should be recognised in this equation. Initially, his solution looked like this:

$$\text{assets} = \text{liabilities} + \text{income} - \text{expenses}$$

Because mathematicians hate minus signs in their equations, he added expenses to both sides, so that it looked like this:

$$\text{assets} + \text{expenses} = \text{liabilities} + \text{income}$$

This methodology gave rise to the so-called double entry book-keeping system, in which anything added to one side of an equation has to have either a matching addition on the other side or a deduction from the same side.

At any point during the trading year, these calculations are used to maintain a trial balance, in which the net balances of all of the accounts is always zero. At the end of the year, the total balances of the income and expenses accounts are cleared by transferring the net income into the liabilities account (the book-keeping entry is debit income, debit expenses).

After this transaction, the trial balance is still zero, but the only balances are on the assets and liabilities accounts. These balances represent the value of the assets being used in the business and the sums owed to the people who have lent to or invested in the business.

The double-entry system was used, with many refinements, for hundreds of years, until by the turn of the 20th century, accounting practice and the views of practitioners varied widely and abuse was commonplace.

The earliest accounting standards, or recommendations on accounting principles, were issued as recently as 1944 by the Institute of Chartered Accountants in England and Wales (ICAEW) which was attempting to codify existing practice and to take account of the many and varied views of practitioners.

The Council of the English Institute issued a statement announcing its intention to develop some accounting standards, with the full co-operation of financial, industrial and commercial representatives, but which would have no legal standing and would not be mandatory. Broadly speaking, they were intended to:

1. reduce the variety of reporting and accounting practices, but not by prescriptive means;
2. demand that accounting policies were included in the disclosure requirements, especially when subjective judgement was being used;
3. demand that any departures from established and widely-used practices were disclosed in the accounts; and
4. establish procedures for ensuring that standards were observed.

The Accounting Standards Committee (ASC) was formed from the various national accountancy bodies in order to define an accounting framework. Their objective was to set out for consultation, discussion and approval:

- accounting definitions and terminology;
- the fundamentals of financial accounting;
- the application of these fundamentals;
- the form and content of financial statements; and
- the presentation of accounts and the disclosures required in them.

In order to begin drafting these standards, research papers were commissioned from individuals and companies describing current global practices, the problems associated with them and suggestions as to how these could be alleviated.

Subcommittees were then asked to prepare first drafts of the new standards, using this research and any other relevant material. The drafts were then circulated to industry bodies, trade associations, companies, firms and individuals who had showed an interest in the subject matter.

Following their responses, full exposure drafts were prepared and circulated again, this time much more widely. Again, following comments received, the Standard Statement of Accounting Practice (SSAP) was drafted and circulated to the various national accountancy bodies for approval, before being published as a standard. If agreement on a draft SSAP could not be reached, a Statement Of Recommended Practice (SORP) was published, which was not mandatory and which only required disclosure if it was departed from in a company's reports and accounts.

Since the advent of the Accounting Standards Board (ASB) in 1989, SSAPs are now called Financial Reporting Standards (FRSs), but the process of establishing them is very similar. Although there have been some issues raised by new thinking or by market developments (eg, goodwill and brands, and financial derivatives) most FRSs strengthen, widen or evolve principles already established in SSAPs. Collectively, these standards are referred to as Generally Accepted Accounting Principals (GAAP).

As stated above, these standards are not enshrined in UK law, but it is intended that, when they are applied, they are more likely to produce accounts that comply with company law. If a company departs from the standards in order to comply with the law, it is obliged to disclose the fact that it has done so. In addition, whenever legal disputes arise from financial matters, the accounting standards are likely to be referred to in the courts, as they are recommended and widely used, and have been the result of wide consultation prior to implementation.

Meanwhile, other non-statutory statements of best practice have been established to cover other areas of company and financial management. Not all of them relate to accounting, but since they relate to disclosure in reports and accounts, they are discussed in this book.

There follows a brief outline of the regulatory environment, and the result of its regulations and standards, the Audited Company Report and Accounts.

3. The Regulatory Environment

3.1 BACKGROUND

Company accounts evolved in response to the need for a common discipline that tracked the flow of money through a business, and, at the end of each accounting period, produced a statement of the profitability and value of that business.

Primarily, they are provided for the shareholders of a company, to inform them about the activities and financial position of the company. Incidentally, they are used by other parties, who provide funding to the company, to inform them about the safety of their investment or financial commitment and the likelihood of repayment. These other parties include creditors, lenders (eg, bankers, bondholders), guarantors and other stakeholders such as employees and suppliers.

Every listed company in the UK must produce an annual report and accounts, and each (except companies exempted under small businesses rules) must have their accounts audited. The directors are responsible under the Companies Acts (the Acts) for preparing the financial statements, and two directors must sign them to indicate that they have been approved by the board.

The directors are responsible for keeping the accounting records of the company in sufficiently good order to show and explain the company's transactions, and they must disclose, with reasonable accuracy, the financial position of the company. The directors must ensure that every balance sheet gives a true and fair view of the company's state of affairs and that the profit and loss account gives a true and fair view of the profit and loss of the company for the accounting period.

However, for the purposes of compliance with the Acts, the expression *true and fair* is not defined in the legislation, nor have accountants or auditors ever defined it. It seems to hinge on matters such as materiality and reasonableness, which are issues of judgement.

Accounts are prepared on the basis of the various accounting standards that exist in the UK and internationally, but audited on the basis of whether they comply with company law. Furthermore, companies can depart from accounting standards if they feel that by doing so, they provide a view that is more true and fair than would have been provided by complying with them (the so-called true and fair override).

An example of this can be found in the WPP Group Plc Reports and Accounts for 2000, in which Note 3 of the Accounting Policies section states that "The financial statements depart from the specific requirement of companies legislation to amortise goodwill over a finite period to give a true and fair view." This is a major departure from US GAAP, in which accounting standards are much more prescriptive, leaving no room for subjective opinions, either by the auditors or the company's accountants and directors, and which are more deeply entrenched in law than those of the UK.

For practical purposes, UK audited report and accounts have some material shortcomings:

- they do not establish the real value of a company, which for practical purposes is the value of all of the ordinary shares in issue multiplied by the share price (ie, the market capitalisation);
- they are published only once per annum, and periodic (usually monthly) management accounts information (quite different to the annual report and accounts) is used to run the business; and
- the profit figure shown in the accounts is not used for corporation taxation purposes, and a separate tax computation has to be produced.

So what is their purpose?

Reports & accounts fulfil several main requirements. They provide comprehensive and accurate information, convey an image of the company and fulfil its legal obligation to provide such information (the statutory accounts).

Given the complexity of modern reports and accounts, their limitations as described above and the fact that very few individual shareholders have the necessary ability to read and understand them, one could ask whether they are of any practical use whatsoever.

In answer to that question, an increasingly small number of individuals own shares directly, and often they are held for reasons other than pure investment. The vast majority of quoted company shares are held by institutions such as pension funds and life insurance companies. Besides having access to the sophisticated analytical skills required, these institutions can also achieve very high portfolio diversification and can thus insulate themselves better from the inherent risks of direct equity investments.

Specialist stock analysts produce reports for their private and institutional clients, and some follow companies or sectors very closely, becoming highly knowledgeable and influential in consequence.

The clients of these analysts use the reports to make their investment decisions, so a critical part of stock market regulation is to ensure that these analysts remain objective and independent.

Furthermore, there are many merger and acquisition transactions and share structure changes by listed companies which are sponsored by merchant banks and subject to extensive due diligence investigations by reporting accountants, who have the skills and experience required to dig their way through reports and accounts in order to ascertain whether the company is financially sound.

The conduct of these transactions is heavily regulated and there are strict rules as to what the documents and circulars must contain.

With the annual audit a further regulatory requirement, there is a battery of experts continually reviewing the accounts in an effort to ensure transparency and probity in company reporting.

3.2 COMPANIES ACTS

There have been a number of major Companies Acts, starting in 1948, and continuing in 1967, 1976 and 1981. This legislation is cumulative and subsequent acts have either added to or amended earlier ones. These acts were consolidated into the Companies Act of 1985, which was added to in 1989 and subsequently. Company Law is continuously amended, and recent legislation (The Companies [Amendment] [No. 2] Act 1999 & The Company Law Enforcement Bill 200) cover late filing of accounts and the establishment of the Office of the Director of Corporate Enforcement.

Broadly speaking, the acts require directors to prepare annual accounts as at the date of the company's financial year-end. These accounts require a balance sheet and a profit and loss (P&L) account that show a true and fair view of the company's financial health, as at the end of its financial year. If by following the detailed accounting and disclosure requirements of the legislation, a company fails to give a true and fair view, the directors must provide additional information in the financial statements or a note to the accounts to ensure that a true and fair view is thus given.

The Acts further require that at a general meeting, the directors present to the company (effectively, the shareholders) a copy of the audited accounts in respect of each accounting reference period; and that a copy of these accounts is filed at Companies House. Both the general meeting and the filing must occur within 7 months of the year-end for listed companies and within 10 months for a private limited company.

As already stated, UK and international accounting standards have no basis in company law per se.

3.3 STANDARD SETTING

The Companies Acts were designed to introduce a legal framework for the preparation of reports & accounts, but they only require certain outcomes from the accounts, eg, that the accounts show a true and fair view of the state of the company's finances. What they don't do is explain how these outcomes should be achieved.

This task was left to the accountancy profession, which dealt with the responsibility by establishing accounting standards, each of which examines a certain feature of the accounts, discusses the issues relating to accounting for it, and provides recommended accounting treatments. These standards have proliferated as business and finance have become more complex and global competition has intensified, with a corresponding increase in pressure on companies to perform.

The ASB was established in 1989 for two reasons:

1. in recognition that the SSAPs that preceded it were not suitable for the increasingly complex transactions emerging in the 1990s (mainly derivatives); and
2. to try to eliminate the "appalling abuses of the 1980s." (Sir David Tweedie, Chairman of the ASB).

The ASB was founded to carry out work on a conceptual accounting framework, designed to achieve consistent accounting standards. In March 1999, for consultation purposes, the ASB published a draft of its Statement of Principles for Financial Reporting, which set out the principles that the ASB believed should underlie the preparation and presentation of company accounts. The statement was intended to assist the process of establishing financial reporting standards on a clear and consistent basis.

The statement was based on the Framework for the Preparation and Presentation of Financial Statements issued by the International Accounting Standards Committee (IASC) in 1990, which itself was based on the Statement of Financial Accounting Concepts issued in the USA by the Federal Accounting Standards Board (FASB) between 1978 and 1985.

The principles outlined in these various statements are now used widely by accounting standard setters in the UK, the USA, Canada, Australia and New Zealand (the so-called G4 plus 1 group of standard setters). Although there is a strong consistency in the approach being used, there is still much debate not only about its validity but also about the detail of the individual standards. In the UK, the process being used to release new standards is very lengthy, and causes much debate and professional differences of opinion.

Typically, the ASB issues discussion papers, followed by discussion drafts and exposure drafts, augmented by working and progress papers, interspersed with occasional papers, followed by full Financial Reporting Exposure Drafts (FREDs). Following extensive consultation with bodies such as the accounting profession, the Stock Exchange, the Confederation of British Industry (CBI) and the Hundred Group (a group of around 100 public companies selected from a broad range of sectors, which is heavily involved in the consultation process around new accounting standards), these are eventually released as FRSs. Each FRS is subject to further review, update and examination by other bodies, and exemption from it is frequently granted to various companies or sectors in which its rigid application would cause problems.

In addition to the ASB's own work on standards, it runs an Urgent Issues Task Force (UITF), which examines problem areas with standards, and releases abstracts for discussion and consultation, which lead eventually to any necessary changes being made to the FRSs. (Further information on these publications can be obtained from the ASB's website at www.asb.org.uk.)

In addition, the various national and international standard setting bodies comment on each other's discussion papers and draft standards.

To strengthen the regulatory regime, another body, called the Financial Reporting Review Panel (FRRP), has been established, which is tasked with reviewing published reports and accounts and checking them for compliance with the requirements of company law and with accounting standards. The FRRP has the power to censure and fine miscreants and to compel them to restate their accounts.

When these bodies are added to the ICAEW Financial Reporting Committee, there is clearly a plethora of standard setters and watchdogs, all trying to ensure that reports and accounts are as clear and robust as possible. The IASC is straining to get its standards accepted worldwide, but in addition to the many national differences in areas such as legal infrastructure, practice and precedent, there are other potentially conflicting demands, especially the requirements of the various stock exchange regulators, such as SEC in the USA and the Financial Services Authority (FSA) in the UK.

However, international standard setters are now on a mission, not just to harmonise and codify national standards, but to overhaul them completely based on supposedly common principles and frameworks.

The outcome has been a strong trend towards ever longer and more complicated standards that attempt to address all of the potential issues in every country and business sector and all the potential problems in applying them. Familiar accounting concepts such as prudence, matching and realised profit are now regarded as very old fashioned. There is little hope that even codification is going to be possible (especially in complex and problematic areas such as derivatives, leases, deferred tax and pensions accounting) thus complicating international harmonisation.

Nowadays, the emphasis is on economic reality, on the real risks and rewards of ownership, on substance over form and on the clear definitions of assets and liabilities, involving an increased use of discounting and mark-to-market valuation techniques as the bases of measurement. Increasingly, performance is judged on increments in balance sheet values, rather than merely profit and loss or cash flow, although profit is still the most important measure.

3.4. THE LISTING RULES (PURPLE BOOK)

Before 1 May 2000, the Listing Rules and the Takeover Code for UK public companies were the responsibility of the UK Listing Authority (UKLA), which was contained within the London Stock Exchange (LSE). The Listing Rules were set out in what was known as the Yellow Book and the Takeover Code was set out in the Blue Book.

From 1 May 2000 the FSA replaced the LSE as the Listing Authority for UK stocks, and the Yellow and Blue Books have now been combined into the Purple Book. The contents of the Purple Book were almost exactly the same as the Blue and Yellow books following the changes, but the FSA is now responsible for the ongoing process of engaging in consultation on possible future changes.

The Purple Book sets out the rules with which public companies must comply in order to obtain and maintain their listing on the LSE (the Listing Rules) and the rules that apply to merger, acquisition and disposal transactions (the Takeover Code). These rules govern:

- the admission to listing on the LSE;
- the continuing obligations of listed companies (otherwise known as issuers) both in maintaining their listing and in the conduct of merger, acquisition and disposal transactions; (the old Blue Book rues);
- the procedures for the enforcement of the rules and obligations; and
- the suspension and/or cancellation of listings.

The rules take into account the mandatory requirements of the UK Financial Services and Markets Act (FSMA) of December 2001, the relevant European Community Directives, any additional requirements mandated by the FSA in its role as the competent authority in relation to securities covered by the FSMA, and any similar requirements relating to other listed securities.

In addition to making the listing rules, under Section 73(2) of the FSMA, the UKLA is also responsible for giving general guidance and establishing the policies and principles that will be applied in carrying out its responsibilities under the Act.

The directors of companies seeking a listing for their securities are responsible for preparing and submitting the relevant application to the UKLA, and the UKLA decides whether the application complies with its requirements.

Broadly speaking, their responsibility is to ensure that the listing rules provide an appropriate level of investor protection, that UK companies and business will thereby be able to gain ready access to finance from listed financial markets, and that the integrity and competitiveness of UK financial markets is maintained.

In summary, the chapters in the Purple Book deal with the following subject headings:

1. compliance and enforcement of the rules, and the powers and sanctions (penalties such as suspension and/or cancellation of listings) available to the UKLA;
2. responsibilities of sponsors of listed security issues (eg, merchant banks);
3. eligibility criteria for obtaining a listing;
4. the various methods available for bringing securities to listing (eg, flotations, IPOs, placings, rights issues);
5. requirement to produce prospectuses or equivalent offering documents (or the terms of any exemption from this requirement), all of which must be approved by the UKLA;
6. provision of the information required in listing particulars;
7. listing application procedures;
8. requirements for the publication and marketing of listing particulars;

9. continuing obligations of listed companies, relating to the disclosure of general information about the company and its financial condition, and any changes to its capital structure or major interests in its shares. This chapter also signposts the requirement for the timely and accurate publication of relevant financial information;
10. rules relating to merger, acquisition or disposal transactions undertaken by listed companies (ie, the rules formerly set out in the Stock Exchange Blue Book;
11. rules and safeguards to protect investors concerning related party transactions (ie, transactions of listed companies with current or former directors, substantial shareholders and/or their associates);
12. requirements for the publication of financial information, including comparative financial tables, auditors' reports, profit forecasts, pro-forma financial information, interim and preliminary financial statements and the annual reports and accounts. This chapter also includes the rules covering compliance with the combined code of corporate governance, which is appended to the listing rules but is not part of them;
13. provisions for the contents and the approval of certain documents relating to the listed company, such as memoranda and articles of association, trust deeds or deeds of title and employee share schemes;
14. requirements relating to the issue of circulars, both those of a routine nature and those that require shareholder approval, the latter of which must also contain a recommendation from the directors;

15. requirements for the purchase by a listed company of its own securities;
16. continuing obligations of the directors of listed companies, including disclosures about their dealings in the company's securities, which are covered by a model code appended to the rules;
17. modifications of the rules for overseas companies seeking a listing on the LSE, including the mutual recognition provisions relating to the approval of the listing documents by the relevant competent authority of the company;
18. rules relating to the valuation reports of property companies;
19. rules relating to the treatment of proven or provable reserves for mining or other extraction companies;
20. rules relating to the provision of information by scientific research-based companies (eg, financial track record);
21. rules relating to investment and property investment companies;
22. rules relating to securities issued by public sector bodies;
23. rules relating to specialist debt securities (including Eurobonds and securitised derivatives) and certificates representing securities (eg, warrants);
24. See Chapter 23 above;
25. rules regarding innovative high growth companies without the required track record to qualify for listing under the other provisions of the Purple Book;
26. requirements for venture capital trusts, which are related to other rules concerning investment trusts; and

27. requirements for listing of securities issued by strategic investment trusts.

As with the financial reporting standards, the listing rules are subject to continuous refinement as issues arise or the rules are tested in court or by precedent. They are available on the FSA's web-site at www.fsa.gov.uk/pubs/ukla/

3.5 AUDIT

An audit is a legal requirement for all but the smallest limited companies in the UK. An audit is a work-supported opinion given by a specialist, independent third party accountant, licensed to practice as an auditor in the UK, on the company's accounting records, and implicitly at least, on whether these records meet the requirements of the Companies Acts.

The Auditor's report is contained within the accounts and follows a standard format, containing:

- a statement that the audit has been carried out in accordance with current auditing standards;
- a report that the auditors have thereby formed an opinion;
- a statement that the opinion of the auditors is that the financial statements either do or do not meet the Act's requirements (implicitly and explicitly); and
- the date and signature of the auditor.

A number of legal cases, starting with Caparo in 1991, have tried to clarify the duty of care of an auditor, ie, establish to whom the auditor is legally liable. Caparo Plc acquired a company which was subsequently found to have mis-stated its accounts. Caparo sued the company's auditors Touche Ross, but the House of Lords upheld Touche Ross' argument that it had no duty of care to Caparo as it was a third party that was not a shareholder at the time the accounts had been signed and issued. In other words, auditors only have a duty of care to existing shareholders at the time the accounts are issued.

This excludes by definition anyone reading the financial statements with a view to making an investment in the company, and any lenders to or creditors of the company.

The original judgement has been extended and refined, but its basic import had not changed until the Bannerman case in July 2002. In this Scottish case, a small firm of auditors was successfully sued by the Royal Bank of Scotland (RBS), which claimed that it had relied on audited accounts when making a lending decision. Although RBS was not a shareholder at the time of the loan, the Scottish courts decided that Touche Ross did have a duty of care in this case.

This judgement appears to have overturned Caparo and has led audit firms to seek to include disclaimers in their reports to the effect that they neither accept nor assume any responsibility for any "other purpose" to which the accounts may be put, or to any "other person" to whom the reports and accounts are shown. It is not clear whether this case will go to appeal, nor is it clear to whom the disclaimer is addressed or who these other people are, but such attempts to use a disclaimer this wide will have sent the wrong message to audit clients.

It is clear why auditors seek to limit their potential liability from the collapse of their clients. Many company failures in the past have been laid almost entirely at the door of the auditors, and of course the best recent example is Enron, which collapsed in 2002, following a huge fraud, subsequently taking its auditor Arthur Andersen with it. However, in this case the company was responsible for the fraud and the auditors did not have a responsibility to detect fraud. Arthur Andersen collapsed as a result of its having broken the law by obstructing justice through the destruction of documents, not because it failed to spot the fraud.

There have been many examples of companies with clean audit reports subsequently collapsing, almost always due to the company having concealed vital or material information from the auditor. Even though the auditor is the paid servant of the directors, and often receives huge income from consultancy services to their audit clients, no-one would suggest that an auditor would willingly be complicit in a fraud. Indeed, there have been many occasions when auditors have qualified accounts, resigned or blown the whistle as soon as they have detected fraud or malpractice.

Furthermore, there have also been a number of cases in which administrators or liquidators of bankrupt companies have successfully sued auditors on behalf of the shareholders at the time of the collapse, notably the Barings Bank case. It is expected that the shareholders of Enron will mount a class action law suit against both the company and Arthur Andersen.

3.6 CORPORATE GOVERNANCE (THE COMBINED CODE)

Part of the response to the excesses and accounting scandals of the 1980s was a development in the area of corporate governance, which concerns the operational control and ethical standards to be applied by the directors of public companies. There were a series of reports that covered areas such as internal financial control, executive remuneration and risk management.

The Combined Code on Corporate Governance was issued in June 1998, and brought together the previous raft of codes that had been issued since 1992, which were:

- Cadbury
  The Cadbury Code on Corporate Governance, published in December 1992, was a ground-breaking effort to introduce the principle of good corporate governance into listed companies. It made recommendations on matters such as regular board meetings, division of responsibilities at the head of a company and the desirability of non-executive directors. It stated that the directors had a duty to maintain systems of control and to report on their effectiveness to the shareholders. It raised the question of who should be leading, organising and co-ordinating risk management activities and recommended that compliance with the code was made compulsory for listed companies.

- Rutteman
  The Rutteman guidance was published in 1994 and concerned the implementation of internal financial controls.
- Greenbury
  The Greenbury Code on Directors' remuneration published in 1995 recommended the establishment of remuneration committees, and set out basic standards for the setting and disclosure of directors' remuneration, requiring its disclosure in notes to reports and accounts. The main elements of this code are retained in the new combined code.
- Hampel
  In June 1998, Sir Ronald Hampel issued the first combined code of corporate governance principles, which said, inter alia, that the board should be supplied with information to enable it to discharge its responsibilities. It also updated the requirements for more openness at board meetings and strengthened protection of shareholders' rights.
- Turnbull
  The Turnbull Committee produced the latest Combined Code in June 1998, sweeping up and enlarging the previous codes. The main requirements of the Turnbull Report are:
  - Provision D2
    The Board should maintain a sound system of internal control to safeguard shareholders' investments and the company's assets.

- ○ Provision D2.1
  The directors should, at least annually, conduct a review of the effectiveness of the company's system of controls and should report to the shareholders that they have done so. The review should cover all controls, including financial, operational and compliance controls and risk management.
- Provision D2.2
  Companies which do not have an internal audit function should, from time to time, review the need for one.

On 20 April 1999, the ICAEW published its consultative guidance from the Turnbull working party on the implementation of the new internal control requirements of the Combined Code, and these are now compulsory for accounting periods that ended on or after 23 December 2000.

In addition to setting out the responsibilities of the directors, the Code sets out minimum disclosure requirements confirming that in the view of the directors, internal controls have been implemented and that, although these controls can only provide reasonable but not absolute assurance, they are working satisfactorily. The system of internal controls should include an ongoing process for identifying, analysing and managing key risks. Auditors however, are not required to give an opinion as to their effectiveness.

In themselves, the recommendations of the Code are relatively toothless, but compliance with them is now required by the Purple Book Rules 12.43A (a) and (b).

Listed companies incorporated in the United Kingdom are now required to include in their annual report and accounts:

- a statement of how they have applied the principles set out in Section 1 of the Combined Code, providing sufficient explanation to enable its shareholders to evaluate properly how the principles have been applied;
- a statement as to whether or not they have complied throughout the accounting period with the Code provisions set out in Section 1 of the Combined Code. A company that has not complied with the Code provisions, or complied with only some of the Code provisions or (in the case of provisions whose requirements are of a continuing nature) complied for only part of an accounting period, must specify the Code provisions with which it has not complied, and (where relevant) for what part of the period such non-compliance continued, and give reasons for any non-compliance.

4. Summary of Contents, Structure and Purpose of Reports & Accounts

4.1 PURPOSE

Having stated above that, for day-to-day purposes, reports and accounts appear to serve no practical purpose, and that few shareholders either read or understand them, why are they required by law?

Traditionally, the explanation is that they are required for the following reasons.

a) Consistency and comparability. Shareholders and other users of accounts need to be able to compare the performance of their company both to other companies and also to past performance. If the content and structure of reports and accounts varied widely, and companies were not required to account for things on a consistent basis, any comparison would be impossible.
b) Ease of interpretation. Received wisdom is that standardised information and layout will facilitate public understanding. However, even sophisticated users can sometimes be confused, and, if they are confused, they are likely to assume that something is being hidden from them. Since sophisticated users are often practitioners, they will probably assume that things are being hidden in any event.
c) Accountability and openness. Company directors have a legally binding fiduciary duty (a trusteeship) to their

shareholders. They are responsible for acting in the best interests of the shareholders in the management of their money and of their company. The requirement to present accounts that are uniform in content and structure to the shareholders is regarded as making it more difficult to be dishonest in carrying out this fiduciary duty.

d) Credibility. Clear reporting and accounts should assist the raising of equity (share capital) and debt to finance the company's activities.

4.2 STRUCTURE & CONTENTS

There are four main elements to the reporting aspects of a set of accounts:

1) The primary statements (including Accounting Policies);
2) The Notes;
3) Additional statutory or disclosure requirements; and
4) The auditors report.

The primary statements in a set of accounts are the profit & loss account (P&L), the balance sheet, the cash flow statement and the statement of recognised gains and losses. These are examined in greater detail in Chapter 2, but are introduced in Section 5 below.

There is also a series of notes to the accounts, which contain further information behind the numbers in the primary statements and form part of the accounts.

In addition to these primary statements and notes, further minimum levels of disclosure are required (eg, the chairman's report, the operating and financial review, and a statement of accounting policies). Of these, the Operating and Financial Review, introduced in 1992, is the most interesting.

It is designed to extract and distil the essence of the accounts in a clear narrative form, but while it is required to represent a balanced, detailed commentary on a company's business and finances, the requirement is vague about what should be included. The ASB originally wanted it to be an accounting standard, but because it is not part of the accounts and goes so far beyond existing accounting practice, it is only a voluntary statement and is not enforceable.

This is in stark contrast to the US and Canadian equivalents, where the "management discussion and analysis" section is mandatory. However, because it is mandatory, it is sometimes very brief and uninformative, as opposed to the lengthy and whimsical versions sometimes seen in the UK. Clearly, directors will be much more circumspect in what they say in their operating review when it forms part of the accounts, rather than just being an adjunct to them.

The final element of a company's reports and accounts is the auditor's report. This is usually found at the end of the various directors' reports and just before the financial statements. An audit of a company's accounts is usually a statutory requirement, and the auditor's report states:

- what work they have carried out (usually just a statement to the effect that they have audited the financial statements in the report and accounts);
- the various responsibilities associated with the reports and accounts (that of the company's directors for preparing the accounts and the responsibilities of the auditor under statute, accounting practices, the listing rules and professional ethical guidance);
- the nature of their report which is an opinion as to whether the:
    - accounts give a true and fair view and are properly prepared in accordance with company law;
    - directors' reports are consistent with the financial statements;
    - company has kept proper accounting records, co-operated with the auditor and provided all of the information required to carry out the audit;
    - proper disclosure as required by company law has been made;
- the basis of their audit opinion (which sets out the procedures and guidance used in the work, and how the audit was planned and executed); and
- the text of the said opinion as to whether the accounts show a true and fair view.

The audit does not provide a guarantee that the accounts are accurate, nor that there has been no material misstatement, whether caused by fraud, irregularities or error. It also does not consider whether the board's statements on internal control covers all relevant risks and controls, nor whether its corporate governance, risk management and control procedures are effective. It is also made explicit that the audit work is carried out on a test basis, ie, that sample transactions are reviewed rather than all of them.

5. The Primary Statements

The content and format of the reports and accounts are set out in the Companies Acts, and in addition to the following principal statements to be included, companies must set out the accounting policies used in arriving at the balance sheet and the P&L.

Although the accounting standards are not themselves enshrined in law, they have been formulated (as described in Section 3.3 above) to meet the requirements of the Companies Acts.

For example, there is no legal requirement to account for depreciation, but the Acts require that fixed assets are recorded at their production cost or their purchase price. However, both the accounting and the cash value of these assets will change over time, and in order to show this change, the assets must be depreciated. SSAP 12 was formulated to give guidance as to how this should be achieved.

There is no accounting standard for providing segmental information (ie, sales revenues obtained from different types of business or in different parts of the world) but there is a legal requirement to show separately the turnover and P&L of businesses of two or more classes which, in the opinion of the directors, differ substantially from each other.

These are fine distinctions, but there is scope for directors to diverge from the accounting standards in order to meet the legal requirements contained in the Companies Acts.

In addition to showing a true and fair view of the state of the company's affairs, the Acts also require of reports and accounts that:

- they are prepared on a going concern basis (ie, that the company will be able to continue trading, and be able to meet its financial commitments when they fall due, for at least 18 months after the year end);
- accounting policies are consistently applied from year to year;
- the amounts of any items stated have been determined on a prudent basis (ie, profits must have been realised at the balance sheet date, all liabilities and losses have been taken into account, all income and charges related to the financial year have been taken into account [ie, accounted for on an accruals basis], and there should be no pooling or netting of assets or liabilities);

The primary statements in a set of accounts are the:

1) P&L statement;
2) balance sheet;
3) cash flow statement; and
4) statement of recognised gains and losses.

5.1 THE PROFIT & LOSS STATEMENT

The P&L shows whether an entity is making a profit on its activities by showing the sales revenues in the trading period and deducting the total costs associated with those sales.

There are some important provisos regarding the P&L.

1. It does not show the amount of cash that the company has generated during the year.
2. Only revenue costs are included in the P&L. Revenue costs are those associated with the provision of the goods or services provided and sold, so that a proper estimation of the profit or loss can be made.
   The other type of costs are capital costs, which are incurred in acquiring, improving or developing fixed assets used in the business. These costs are usually capitalised, ie, added to the balance sheet, rather than taken through the P&L. In this way, they become part of the ongoing value of the company rather than being attributed to the provision of the goods or services provided and sold in any given financial year.
3. Following the implementation of FRS 3, exceptional items (which were formerly shown on the P&L after operating profit, ie, below the line) are now included above the line with a note to the accounts stating what the exceptional item was. Only exceptional items relating to the profit or loss on the sale of fixed assets or subsidiary companies are now shown separately on the face of the accounts. FRS 3 (formerly SSAP 6) also

> effectively removed extraordinary items from the face of the accounts, defining them as so extremely rare that they could not think of an example of what sort of transaction might be so defined. Indeed, although the Companies Acts require them to be disclosed, they are not defined.

Finally, all P&L accounts must show the relevant information under the following headings:

- profit and loss on ordinary activities before taxation;
- total dividends payable or proposed; and
- any amounts taken from or added to reserves.

An example is given below of the most common UK format of P&L, taken from the 2001 accounts of Electrocomponents Plc:

Electrocomponents Plc Consolidated Profit & Loss Account	**£m**
Turnover	855.1
Cost of sales	(444.2)
Gross profit	**410.9**
Distribution and marketing expenses	(266.8)
Administration expenses	
before amortisation of goodwill	(13.2)
amortisation of goodwill	(11.6)
	(24.8)
Operating profit	
before amortisation of goodwill	130.9
amortisation of goodwill	(11.6)
	119.3
Exceptional loss on closure	(6.9)
Net interest payable and similar charges	(6.8)
Profit on ordinary activities before taxation	**105.6**
Profit on ordinary activities before taxation, amortisation of goodwill and exceptional loss	**124.1**
Taxation on profit on ordinary activities	(33.0)
Profit on ordinary activities after taxation	72.6
Ordinary dividends	(59.8)
Retained profit for the year	12.8

What this P&L statement reveals is that the company made an operating profit, after writing off some goodwill, of £119.3 million, made pre-tax profits of £105.6 million, it distributed £59.8 million to shareholders and retained £12.8 million in shareholders' funds.

Although on the face of it, these cost headings all look reasonably self-explanatory, there is much scope for judgement to be exercised as to what the appropriate figures are and how they should be set out. A comparative glance at other company accounts will quickly demonstrate how different they can be.

The P&L will be examined in greater detail in Chapter 2 below.

5.2 THE BALANCE SHEET

The Balance Sheet is a statement, a snapshot, as at the financial period end, of a company's assets and liabilities.

Its main function is to give an indication of the financial health of the company, and whether it has sufficient liquidity to pay its debts as they fall due.

The balance sheet is usually divided into two parts: net assets at the top and capital employed (or shareholders' funds) at the bottom. The top section shows what the shareholders' funds have been invested in (the net assets) and the bottom section states where the money to buy those assets came from.

Again, there are some important provisos regarding the balance sheet.

1. It only shows the value of the company in accounting terms. It does not show what the company is worth, nor does it indicate what a potential buyer would or should pay for it, which according to one definition, is the same as what it is worth. Although the figure at the bottom is usually labelled shareholders' funds or similar, it is very rare for the actual value of a company to be the same as the shareholders' funds or net worth.

A much better indication of the value of a quoted company is its market capitalisation, which is its share price multiplied by the number of shares in issue. When the market capitalisation is lower than the net assets in the balance sheet, the company's shares are said to be trading at a discount to net assets, and when it is higher, they are said to be trading at a premium to net assets.

Even the market capitalisation can be a flawed indicator, because if every shareholder tried simultaneously to sell their shares, the value of the shares would certainly drop very quickly before they all managed to sell them, as potential buyers would wonder why they all wanted to sell. On the other hand, when a company receives a takeover bid, the value of the shares usually jumps. Both of these share price reactions can occur without any material change in the accounting value of the net assets, so the value of a quoted company is very much a matter of sentiment rather than accounting.

2. The second proviso is that the balance sheet is only a snapshot of the financial position of the company on one day at the end of the financial year. By the time it has been published, usually between three and six months after the year end, the situation could have changed materially. If this material change is known about before the year end, the company will put an explanatory note in the accounts under 'post-balance sheet events' so that recipients of the accounts are informed of it.

An example is given below of the most common UK format of balance sheet, again taken from the accounts of Electrocomponents Plc:

Electrocomponents Plc Consolidated Balance Sheet	£m
Fixed assets	
Intangible fixed assets	219.7
Tangible fixed assets	133.3
Investments	0.3
	353.3
Current assets	
Stocks	165.3
Debtors	168.9
Investments	6.7
Cash at bank and in hand	10.6
	351.5
Creditors: amounts falling due within one year	(202.1)
Net current assets	**149.4**
Total assets less current liabilities	**502.7**
Creditors: amounts falling due after more than one year	(76.6)
Provisions for liabilities and charges	(9.6)
Net assets	**416.5**
Capital and reserves	
Called up share capital	43.4
Share premium account	34.9
Profit & loss account	338.2
Equity share owners' funds	**416.5**

What this balance sheet is saying is that £416.5 million has been invested in the net assets necessary to run the business, and the cash has either been raised from shareholders (share capital and share premium account) or has been accumulated by the company (profit & loss account).

5.3 THE CASH FLOW STATEMENT

The requirement to publish a cash flow statement was established by FRS 1, and it is designed to analyse the difference between opening and closing cash and overdraft balances.

The requirement was necessary because the P&L does not show cash movement, and because accounting profit (and value, in the balance sheet) can be created through exercising judgement, whereas cash cannot. Cash is an indication of solvency, whereas profit is not. A company either has cash or it doesn't, and if it doesn't have it, it cannot continue to trade. In addition to profit being created by exercising judgement, there are also some elements in the P&L that are not cash, the best example of which is depreciation. Depreciation is deducted from profit but usually, there has been no matching cash outflow.

The cash flow statement shows from where a company has received money and what it has been spent on. Broadly speaking, cash flows arise from trading (operating activities), the purchase and sale of fixed assets (investment), interest and dividends (servicing of finance and returns on investments) and taxation.

The total of these flows is known as the cash flow before financing and shows whether a company is paying its way. Once this total is arrived at, the cash surplus or shortfall is then reconciled to financing, cash and cash equivalents. If the cash flow is negative, the company must raise the cash either by issuing new shares or by increasing long-term borrowings (financing) or by increasing short-term debt or reducing deposits (cash or cash equivalents).

The cash flow statement used to be called the source and application of funds, which although long-winded, is perhaps more redolent of the contents and function of the statement.

An example is given below of the most common UK format of balance sheet, again taken from the accounts of Electrocomponents Plc:

Electrocomponents Plc Consolidated Cash Flow Statement	**£m**
Reconciliation of operating profit to net cash inflow from operating activities	
Operating profit	119.3
Amortisation of goodwill	11.6
Depreciation and other amortisation	21.8
(Increase)/decrease in stocks	0.6
(Increase)/decrease in debtors	(1.4)
(Decrease)/increase in creditors	(9.0)
	142.9
Costs in respect of prior year closures	(0.7)
Net cash flow from operating activities	**142.2**
Cash flow statement	
Net cash flow from operating activities	142.2
Returns on investments	(6.7)
Taxation	(32.6)
Capital expenditure & financial investment	(24.3)
Free cash flow	**78.6**
Acquisition	-
Equity dividends paid	(54.3)
Cash inflow/(outflow) before use of liquid resources and financing	**24.3**
Management of liquid resources	18.2
Financing	
Shares	3.8
Loans	(46.6)
Decrease in cash in the year	**(0.3)**
Reconciliation of net cash flow to movement in net debt	
Decrease in cash	(0.3)
Management of liquid resources	(18.2)
Financing – loans	46.6
Change in net debt relating to cash flows	**28.1**
Translation differences	(7.8)
Decrease/(increase) in net debt for the year	**20.3**
Net (debt) funds at 1 April 2000	(95.8)
Net (debt) funds at 31 March 2001	**(75.5)**

This cash flow statement shows that the company is generating a lot of cash from its operating activities, which translates to a high free cash flow figure (ie, cash flow after net interest, taxation and capital expenditure). After payment of the dividend, cash flow was £24.3 million, which the company used to repay debt, which fell from £95.8m in 2000 to £75.5m in 2001.

5.4 STATEMENT OF RECOGNISED GAINS AND LOSSES

The statement of recognised gains and losses (the STRGL) is the most recent addition to the panoply of statements required in the accounts of public companies in the UK, introduced in 1993 as part of FRS 3. It was introduced to deal with potential movements in reserves in the balance sheet (ie, shareholders' funds) that might not have been shown in the P&L.

Any realised gains or losses on assets or investments (ie, crystallised by a purchase or sale transaction) had to be taken through the P&L, but unrealised gains or losses (eg, revaluation of assets or retranslation of foreign currency loans or investments, or other movements in value not crystallised by a purchase or sale transaction) were previously taken straight to reserves.

Although these movements had previously been disclosed as notes to the accounts, these are not read by everybody and it was therefore felt that these movements in reserves should be shown on the face of the accounts in a separate statement.

[NB On the face of the accounts means included in the primary statements, rather than included in the notes to the accounts.]

An example is given below of the most common UK format of Statement of Total Recognised Gains and Losses, again taken from the accounts of Electrocomponents Plc:

Electrocomponents Plc **Consolidated Statement Of Total Recognised Gains And Losses 2001**	**£m**
Profit for the financial year	72.6
Translation differences	24.4
Total recognised gains and losses relating to the year	97.0

As an added complication, not all changes in reserves are recognised gains or losses (eg, movements in issued share capital or goodwill write-offs) so the accounts must include a note reconciling all other movements in reserves since the previous period end. Therefore, anyone looking at the above accounts will not be able just to add the above figure of £97.0 million to last year's reserves and get the same number as this year's reserves.

Changes in reserves can therefore include both the following items recognised in the P&L and set out in the STRGL:

- profit/loss for the year (profit after tax in the P&L);
- realised translation differences (included in the P&L as set out in the Accounting Policies Statement);

and also those set out in the note on movements in reserves:

- movements in share capital (new shares issued or repaid);
- changes in share premium account (differences between the nominal and issued price of shares);
- goodwill/other intangible asset write-offs;
- unrealised translation differences.

The consensus in the profession is that the STRGL does not have a clear coherent purpose, and is widely used as a dustbin rather than a performance statement, with no consistent basis for recognising items in it.

6. Conclusion

Non-accountants might conclude that accountants have merely pursued esoteric niceties to satisfy their intellectual cravings and professional pride. The result is the aforementioned accounting and financial reporting standards, which, despite their length and erudition, still leave huge scope for interpretation in application, and frequently generate subsequent debate as to whether they have been correctly applied. As business has become more complicated, so has accounting for it.

Furthermore, accounting standards are generally conceived and drafted by standard setters, who tend to take a technical and academic approach to their work, whereas the standards have to be applied by practitioners, who have the unenviable task of trying to establish what the standards mean and how they should account for the transactions undertaken in their business, sometimes advised by their auditors. The auditor then reviews their clients' accounting, giving an opinion as to whether it complies with the standards and produces the desired conformity with company law.

The resulting reports and accounts are reviewed and interpreted by lenders and analysts, who have the highly practical task of deciding what they mean, in order to lend the company money or advise their clients on whether to invest in its shares.

There is a natural tension between the technical need to ensure that transactions are accounted for so that the outcome shows a true and fair view, and the practical need to comprehend the accounts, so that if money is lent or invested there is a reasonable chance of getting it back.

Even an experienced reader of accounts can find it difficult to reconcile and interpret correctly all the figures shown in their various guises. Despite increasing financial regulation, and greater requirement for disclosure and prescription as to method, the considerable scope still allowed for judgement as to which figures are used, and the sometimes very confusing presentation, can make it impossible for the outsider to know what is really going on.

In some ways, the increasing requirement for disclosure has further complicated matters. The cash flow statement and the STRGL, which augment the P&L and the balance sheet, are quite complex statements to understand and to reconcile with the other two statements, and do not really add a great deal to the report and accounts.

In order to understand accounts, it is necessary to understand business, or the accounts will be meaningless. Statutory accounts are prepared solely to comply with company law, they are also PR brochures designed to attract new investors and to reassure existing investors. It should always be remembered, therefore, that companies will do their utmost to ensure that they present their affairs as positively as possible, within the requirements of company law and the accounting standards.

2

PRINCIPAL FINANCIAL STATEMENTS

1. Profit & Loss Account (P&L)

This is the key statement in the accounts in terms of measuring financial performance. As its name suggests, it shows the profit made by a company, which broadly is the sales turnover minus the costs of sales (raw materials, manufacture, delivery, etc) and the cost of running and financing the company (wages, salaries, rent, utilities, interest, etc). Although this sounds deceptively simple, deciding what income the company has received and what the costs actually were is a very intricate science, for which the directors are responsible.

The directors of a company are also responsible to the shareholders for the performance of the company and the safety of their investment. The various and complex accounting standards that have evolved since the innocent days of Paccioli are designed to guide and assist them in arriving at a true and fair view of the financial state of the company.

As stated above, the P&L does not show the amount of cash that the company has generated during the year; only revenue costs are included, not capital expenditure costs. These are charged to the balance sheet, as they relate to fixed assets, plant and machinery, which will remain in the business for future use, rather than working capital assets, which are consumed in the production process. Some items relating to capital assets are charged to the P&L, notably depreciation, which is the replacement cost of, or wear-and-tear on the fixed assets, and the financing and maintenance costs of acquiring and running the fixed assets.

It should be noted that one of the biggest problems with the distinction between capital and revenue costs is that it offers one of the best opportunities for subjective judgement to be used to smooth profits. It is often argued that what should be revenue costs, deducted from the P&L and causing profits to be smaller, are capital costs, which can capitalised (ie, be added to the balance sheet) and depreciated over many years. Needless to say, the impact of being able to take costs over many years, rather than in the year in which they occur, is potentially huge.

In September 2002, one of the companies at the centre of the US accounting scandals, WorldCom, announced that it had overstated profits by more than $4 billion as a result of treating revenue costs as capital costs. It took the $4 billion hit to its profits when it had to write off the "capital assets" it had subsequently accumulated through this fraudulent accounting.

By taking revenue costs as capital costs, a "double-whammy" effect is achieved. The costs do not come out of profit but are added to asset values, making the accounting value of a company appear larger as well as the profits appear higher.

To illustrate this, imagine that Worldcom had spent £10 million on paper clips in one year, but added this amount to its fixed assets instead of charging it to the P&L. In addition to the P&L having been overstated by £10 million, net assets have also been overstated by £10 million, because paper clips aren't worth anything to this company or its shareholders.

As further illustration, a property development company might state that a proportion of its overhead costs (ie the cost of running the company) should be added to the cost of developing properties, because head office staff costs, stationery, rent, utilities, etc are incurred in the business of developing the properties, so these costs can be capitalised as part of the cost of development.

Chemicals and pharmaceuticals companies spend huge amounts of money researching new products, and many of the ostensible revenue costs of so doing are added to the capital values of the brands thus generated. Some companies have even attempted to capitalise redundancy costs incurred during the start-up phase of a new subsidiary business.

This is similar to the process used by British banks during the various third world debt crises of the 1980s. When countries defaulted on their interest payments, the banks would lend them the money to pay the interest, although obviously the cash would never leave the bank. This not only inflated the banks' profits (as the interest income would be higher than their cost of funds) but also a non-performing loan would have been reclassified as a performing loan and the banks' assets got larger, because to banks, loans are assets.

The key elements of the P&L are as follows.

1.1 OPERATING ACTIVITIES (PROFIT BEFORE INTEREST AND TAX)

1.1.1 Sales turnover

Gross or net sales are shown, net of VAT or any other sales taxes. They should be sales made to unrelated third parties and should not include any inter-company sales, which will be disclosed elsewhere in the accounts.

The sales figure is accompanied by a note to the accounts setting out the segmental information relating to the sales figure, by class of business and geographical turnover, and by source and origin.

Class of business refers to the different operating divisions or subsidiaries a company may have within it. For example, the BOC Group Plc shows turnover for the year to 30 September 2000 in a matrix under the following geographical and sector headings:

	Continuing Operations						
	Gases and related products	Vacuum technology	Distribution services	Sub-total	Discontinued operations	Total group by origin	Total group by destination
	£m	£m	£m	£m	£m	£m	£m
2000							
Europe	603.1	152.1	225.3	980.5		980.5	948.9
Americas	931.0	308.9		1,239.9		1,239.9	1,160.6
Africa	500.8			500.8		500.8	499.9
Asia/Pacific	1,058.8	97.7	1.1	1,157.6		1,157.6	1,269.4
	3,093.7	558.7	226.4	3,878.8		3,878.8	3,878.8
1999							
Europe	605.9	94.7	251.6	952.2		952.2	943.4
Americas	821.1	185.1		1,006.2		1,006.2	963.2
Africa	386.7			386.7		386.7	386.7
Asia/Pacific	903.1	61.0	2.4	966.5		966.5	1,018.3
	2,716.8	340.8	254.0	3,311.6		3,311.6	3,311.6
1998							
Europe	667.5	104.8	312.4	1,084.7	76.7	1,161.4	1,120.5
Americas	831.8	177.0		1,008.8	114.3	1,123.1	1,076.6
Africa	333.9			333.9		333.9	335.4
Asia/Pacific	864.1	41.3	1.5	906.9	24.6	931.5	1,017.4
	2,697.3	323.1	313.9	3,334.3	215.6	3,549.9	3,549.9

This information is repeated for the previous two financial years, so that the reader can see the extent to which the global reach of the company is evolving. If a company's strategy is global diversification and/or focus on specific business sectors, this kind of analysis shows how the strategy is progressing.

At a glance, this table shows that Vacuum Technology grew very rapidly between 1999 and 2000, by over 60% across all of the markets in which it is sold. Gases and related products have grown much more slowly, with the best performances from Asia/ Pacific and Africa. It also shows that there is little cross-border activity in the group, with sales by origin and destination being very similar, indicating that costs are incurred in the same territory as the sales are made.

From the segmental analysis, it can be seen that profit margins are more or less the same across these business sectors, but when PBIT is compared to the capital employed in these sectors, the picture is very different, with Vacuum Technology producing around twice the profit and Distribution producing two and a half times as much as Gases and Related Products.

In addition to the above comments about the possibility of blurring the distinction between revenue and capital costs, the sales turnover line also presents opportunities for creative accounting, or more specifically, premature income recognition.

Company law requires companies to be prudent in preparing their accounts, and one aspect of the requisite prudence is that income should not be recognised before it has become real. Premature recognition of income in the accounts is not permitted, but there is scope in some types of business for this to occur.

Long term service or consultancy contracts represent one of the biggest opportunities for enlarging revenues, because a customer is committed to purchasing goods or services over a period of time. However, these contracts are usually conditional to some degree, which is why it is imprudent to account for the sales before they become real. Most leases are long-term in nature and leasing companies have many opportunities to recognise income prematurely.

In 1990, Atlantic Computers collapsed, bringing down its parent company, B&C Plc, a company once valued at more than £1 billion on the stock market. Atlantic was signing 7 year leases with its customers, then signing a second agreement which gave the customer the right to *flex* the lease after three years (ie, terminate the old lease, upgrade the equipment, providing that it was for a more expensive piece of equipment than the original piece, and engage in a new lease) or to terminate the lease after 5 years leaving the remaining two years' instalments unpaid (the *walk*). It then sold the leases to external funders, who included some very large and well-known banks, and in many cases it did not tell them about the flex or walk agreements.

Atlantic accounted for the sale value of the lease as revenue and, after deducting the cost of the equipment, it took all of the profit in the accounting period in which the lease was sold, rather than prudently over the life of the lease. It never accounted for the potential liabilities under the flex or walk agreements. The DTI inspectors appointed to investigate the collapse concluded that if Atlantic had accounted prudently for its business, it would never have made a profit from the day it was founded to the day it collapsed. However, in its lifetime, it had been floated once, making multi-millionaires of a number of its founders, and had then been bought by B&C for over £400 million.

In early 2002, the giant US energy company Enron collapsed after it was discovered that, in addition to hiding large liabilities off-balance sheet in special purpose vehicles, it had been prematurely recognising large chunks of income on long-term energy contracts. In July 2002, the US photocopier company Xerox admitted overstating its sales revenues by $6.4 billion between 1997 and 2001, through the simple expedient of taking immediate sales credit for leased equipment, rather than booking it to sales over the life of the lease.

Other examples of profit overstatement in recent years include:

- Kwik-Fit, the UK tyre and exhaust centre (manipulating stock accruals by understating liabilities for supplier payments);
- Wickes, the UK-based DIY company (accounting up front for golden hello payments ie, advance payments on signing of new supplier contracts); and
- Allied Carpets (pre-dispatching -ie, booking as sales revenue the cost of carpets ordered but not paid for).

1.1.2 Stock

Stock is an important component of the cost of sales figure deducted from the P&L. It is a complicated area in which judgement must be applied to arrive at a reasonable and accurate figure.

Some of the stock in place at the start of the financial year, which gets used during the year, may have been paid for before the start of that year. Any stock left at the end of the year may have been paid for during the year, but not used. Therefore it is necessary to calculate how much was actually paid for the stock that was used during the year being accounted for.

Theoretically, the calculation of the amount of stock used during the year is easy:

Opening stock + Purchases = Stock available
Stock available - Closing stock = Stock used during the year

However, there are complications and choices once a company has worked out how much stock it used and how much is left at the end of the year.

Closing stock was valued at the previous year-end, so this figure will comprise the opening stock figure for the current year. The consistency requirement in the Acts will usually demand that the same valuation method is used to value closing stock for the current year. The three main choices of valuation method are:

- First in first out (FIFO)
  This method assumes that stock will be efficiently rotated through the warehouse and that it will be used in the order in which it arrived. Any stock remaining at the year-end is assumed to have cost what the most recent delivery cost.
- Average cost
  This method takes the number of deliveries multiplied by the price of each delivery, and simply averages the cost for all stock used during the year.

- Last in first out (LIFO)
  This is the least-used method in the UK, as it implies that old stock is left sitting around, and only the most recently delivered is used. Any remaining stock is valued at the prices that it would have cost for however many deliveries were made at the beginning of the year to build that stock.

Like depreciation choices, these different methods can have a dramatic effect on the P&L (cost of sales) and the balance sheet (working capital asset values). For example:

Date	Item	Units	Unit Cost	Total Cost
01-Jan	Opening stock	500	12.50	6,250
01-Mar	Purchase	450	12.00	5,400
01-Jun	Purchase	500	11.50	5,750
01-Sep	Purchase	590	11.50	6,785
01-Nov	Purchase	550	11.00	6,050
01-Dec	Purchase	475	10.50	4,988
	Totals	3,065		35,223
31-Dec	Closing stock	625		

	Unit cost for valuation	*Closing stock units*	*Closing stock value*	*Cost of sales*
FIFO	10.50	625	6,563	28,660
Average	11.49	625	7,182	28,040
LIFO	12.50	625	7,813	27,410

Although the numbers in this example are not large, there is a 19% difference between the FIFO and LIFO closing stock values, and a 4.5% difference in the resulting cost of sales calculation, with the FIFO figure being the larger. These numbers applied to a large company could be highly material and could make a big difference to asset values.

Although by definition, the aggregate of the closing stock value and the cost of sales figures are always the same for all three methods, if it were possible for companies to convince their auditors that they should elect for one method rather than another, they could chose which looked the best: either a low cost of sales to boost the P&L or a low stock figure in the balance sheet.

1.1.3 Operating costs

As the name suggests, operating costs are the costs of materials, labour and overheads that are incurred in the production and sale of the goods and services to which the turnover figure apples. Again, these figures are quoted net of all sales taxes, such as VAT.

Under EU accounting rules, reflected in the Acts, there are two approved formats for the presentation of these elements of the P&L:

a) specific cost areas on which the money has been spent (eg, salaries/wages, raw materials, establishment, other overheads, etc); or
b) production activities on which the money has been spent (eg, cost of sales, administration, selling and distribution).

The key performance indicators (operating profit, profit before interest and tax, profit before tax, profit after tax and retained profit) are the same whichever presentation is used.

Picking up the BOC accounts for 30 September 2000, the P&L looks like this:

The BOC Group Plc **Group profit and loss account** Years ended 30 September	**After exceptional items** **£m**
Turnover	
Continuing operations	3,878.8
Discontinued operations	-
Turnover including share of joint venture and associates	3,878.8
Less share of turnover of joint ventures	(258.0)
Less share of turnover of associates	(41.1)
Turnover of subsidiary undertakings	3,579.7
Cost of sales	(2,088.7)
Gross profit	1,491.0
Net operating expenses	(991.4)
Operating profit	
Continuing operations	499.6
Discontinued operations	-
Operating profit of subsidiary undertakings	499.6
Share of operating profit of joint ventures	48.1
Share of operating profit of associates	8.5
Total operating profit including share of joint ventures and associates	556.2
Profit on disposal of health care discontinued business	12.5
Profit on disposal of business - continuing operations	-
Profit on ordinary activities before interest	568.7
Interest (net)	(111.5)
Profit on ordinary activities before tax	457.2
Tax on profit on ordinary activities	(103.7)
Profit on ordinary activities after tax	353.5
Minority interest – equity	(27.1)
Profit for the financial year	326.4
Dividends – equity	(170.2)
Surplus for the financial year	156.2

Although there are some minor differences in terminology, the content and structure of this statement is very similar to that of Electrocomponents above.

In preparing the operating costs for the P&L, the starting point is the total of cash paid out in respect of producing the goods and services being sold. Some adjustments then need to be made to those figures, which are:

- provisions;
- accruals;
- depreciation;
- stock; and
- prepayments.

Each of these will now be examined in greater detail.

1.1.4 Provisions

Provisions are charged to the P&L in respect of future costs that may occur relating to the trading during the financial year being accounted for. These provisions are likely to include, inter alia:

- bad or doubtful debts;
- stock obsolescence;
- rationalisation or restructuring;
- warranties and guarantees; and
- litigation.

The objective of these provisions is prudence, which is one of the key requirements of the Companies Acts. It would be imprudent of a company to ignore the possibility of future costs arising from known situations during the year, and to state profits and pay dividends accordingly.

Provisions can be made individually or generally. For example, a company could assess the likelihood of each individual debtor not paying up, and provide for all monies owed by that debtor. Alternatively, they could take the view that, as bad debts have run at, say 5% for the previous 5 years, they will do so again, and they could provide for 5% of the outstanding debtors at the year end.

Provisions are made as to 'likely' future costs, so judgement is again called for in establishing the figure to be charged. Provisioning provides many opportunities for moving profit from one year to the next. By increasing provisions above what is strictly required of prudence, profits for the year can be reduced, and when written back the following year, they will inflate profits for that year.

If the directors have forecast that profits will grow at 5% per annum, and they make 8% in the current year, they may increase the general provision by a sufficient amount to reduce the profit to 5%. If their trading position deteriorates in the following year, they will only need to make 2% because they could write back or release the previous year's overprovision into the P&L to bring them back up to their target of 5%. This is called profit smoothing, and helps management to demonstrate that a company is growing progressively, through the good times and the bad, although what they are really doing is storing profit in the balance sheet for use in future years when times may be hard.

In the bad old days of acquisition accounting in the early 1990s, provisions, known as pre-acquisition write downs, were widely used by companies to manipulate their future profits.

On making an acquisition, a company would announce that it was prudently writing down the assets of the acquired company, either to bring their value in line with those of the acquirer, or to adjust them to current rather than historic values. These were often known as big-bath provisions. This write-down would be taken to the shareholders' funds, not via the P&L. There were three consequences:

1. the acquirer could gradually release the provisions, which would go back into the P&L, thus inflating it beyond what had been achieved by its trading during the year;
2. because the book value of the assets was reduced, the subsequent depreciation charges was also lower, and profit was therefore higher; and
3. on any subsequent sale of the subsidiary, the book value was subtracted from the sale price to calculate the profit on disposal, which could then be shown in the P&L.

The current rules under FRS3 are that reorganisation provisions must go through the P&L, so that they are more visible and cannot be used to manipulate future profits to the same extent.

1.1.5 Accruals

Accruals are adjustments for expenses that relate to the current year, but for which the bills will not arrive until after the year-end, the classic example being utility bills. Since electricity will have been used during the financial year, but the bill may not arrive until 2 months after the year-end, an accrual for the month's worth of electricity will give a better indication of the costs incurred in production during the year.

1.1.6 Depreciation

Depreciation is the charge of the P&L to allow for the wearing out (and implicitly the subsequent replacement cost) of assets used during the financial year. It is not a cash cost, and is therefore one of the larger items in the reconciliation between cash-flow and profit. Naturally, judgement is required to decide what the depreciation policy will be.

When calculating depreciation, the directors must take account of the original cost, the projected life of the asset and its potential residual value.

The first decision is the useful life of the asset. As already stated, brands can be written off over 40 years, and certain land and property assets are not depreciated at all. At the other end of the spectrum, consumer goods in sectors subject to rapid product development and obsolescence can realistically be written off in a single year (eg, personal computers, audio-visual equipment).

Obviously, the longer the period over which an asset is used, the lower the depreciation charge and therefore the higher the profit, but while directors have a degree of latitude over these matters, their over-riding objective must be prudence.

The second decision is residual value, which is the value of the asset at the point in time that the owner wishes to dispose of it. This is a major consideration for leasing companies, which must factor residual value into their lease payments to ensure that when the primary period of the lease ends, the asset is worth more than the difference between its original cost and the amount that has been recovered in primary rentals.

This is always a tricky judgement, because depreciation is only an accounting equivalent of obsolescence, whereas in the real world, assets are usually losing their value much faster than companies are writing them off. This loss of value, or obsolescence, is almost always associated with technological or market changes, where models are continually being enhanced or replaced, and quantum leaps in technology may occur.

The final consideration is the method of accounting for depreciation, usually chosen from four main options:

1. straight line, in which the annual charge is cost less residual value, divided by the number of years over which the asset will be used;
2. reducing balance, in which the same percentage of the asset's book value is charged each year, to try to achieve the correct residual value when the time comes to write the asset off;

3. sum of the digits, which gives a result somewhere between the above two methods.
   This method is used extensively in the leasing business, as it reflects equipment depreciation patterns more accurately in that it starts rapidly then tails off.
   The calculation involves adding the digits in the number of years for which the asset will be used, and dividing the asset value by the number of years, the highest first. If an asset will be used for 5 years, the sum of the digits is 1 + 2 + 3 + 4 + 5 = 15. The annual charge on an asset costing £100,000 and being depreciated to 10% of its value is therefore:

Year of charge	*Calculation*	*Annual charge*	*Book value*
			£100,000
Year 1	5/15 * £100,000	£30,000	£70,000
Year 2	4/15 * £100,000	£24,000	£46,000
Year 3	3/15 * £100,000	£18,000	£28,000
Year 4	2/15 * £100,000	£12,000	£16,000
Year 5	1/15 * £100,000	£6,000	£10,000

4. usage basis, which depreciates assets according to how many units have been produced from them, or the elapsed time or distance for which the asset has been utilised. This method would be applied to manufacturing plant designed for a pre-determined life, such as dies, which are precision machined and wear beyond design tolerances after a known number of uses. The latter method would be appropriate for aircraft, where engine hours and take-

off/landing cycles are important factors in the design life of each aircraft. Also, racing car parts are changed after they have attained their optimum target mileage.

1.1.7 Prepayments

Prepayments are perhaps the easiest P&L adjustments to understand, as the term means exactly what it says. They are adjustments to payments that have been made during the year in advance of the goods or services being received, such as licence fees, insurance premiums, subscriptions, etc. For example, if a company paid an annual insurance premium three months before its year end, it would charge one quarter of the cost to the P&L and three quarters would be debited to prepayments.

This "adding back" of the proportion of a cash payment relating to post-year end costs has the effect of increasing profit. In that sense, repayments are the opposite of accruals, which bring charges into the P&L for payments that have not yet been made, but for which some element of the goods or services has been received.

1.1.8 Currency adjustments

Currency adjustments need to be made for all revenue transactions if foreign currencies are involved. However, certain of these adjustments must be made to the P&L rather than the Balance Sheet, and SSAP 20 is the relevant accounting standard.

Companies generally have four choices as to which foreign currency exchange rate (FX rate) they use in their accounting:

1. the closing rate (the one prevailing on the date of the financial year-end);
2. the average exchange rate (for the relevant financial year);
3. the historical rate (the one prevailing on the date of the relevant transaction); or
4. the hedged rate (the one the company has contracted for with a third party).

SSAP 20 requires companies to account for FX fluctuations on trading transactions through the P&L, because FX exposure is a legitimate cost of production. FX exposures in the balance sheet are treated according to the nature of the underlying assets and liabilities.

In outline, FX gains and losses on monetary assets and liabilities are taken into the P&L. FX gains and losses on non-monetary items (ie, plant, machinery, buildings etc) are taken through shareholders' funds in the balance sheet. This method is used in order to avoid the high volatility in company profits that would be caused as a result of annually having to revalue assets denominated in foreign currencies.

In the case of investments in equities (traded securities) denominated in foreign currencies, the treatment is usually to value them at the exchange rate prevailing at the time the investment was made (historical cost). If an investment has been made with funds borrowed in the same currency as the investment, then the year-end exchange rate can be used to revalue it. Any gain or loss on the investment will be taken to reserves in the balance sheet, where it will off-set the matching gain or loss on the underling currency-denominated debt.

1.2 NON-OPERATING COSTS

The P&L items in Section 1.1.3 relate to operating costs, whereas those that follow relate to non-operating costs, principally taxation and financing.

1.2.1 Returns on investment and servicing of financing (interest)

This global heading refers to net interest, which is interest costs on borrowings less interest income from investments. It is used a lot in performance assessment, for a number of reasons:

- debt servicing costs must be paid, as failure to do so could result in lenders calling in their loans, taking vital liquidity out of the company;
- most loan agreements contain financial covenants which require a company to generate sufficient cash and/or profit to cover net interest expense by a multiplier of some magnitude.

  For example, this covenant might be 'PBIT must be 2.5 times greater than net interest expense.' Should this covenant not be met in the audited accounts, lenders might begin to get concerned and start thinking about calling in the loans, or at the very least, rescheduling or renegotiating them, usually on more onerous terms than before.

  Interest cover is calculated as follows:

$$\frac{\text{PBIT}}{\text{Net interest payable}} \qquad \frac{100}{72.5} \qquad = 1.38 \text{ times}$$

In this example, the borrower would have failed a covenant requiring interest cover of 2.5 times.

- As already stated, profit does not equal cash, and increasingly lenders require interest cover as a function of some measure of 'free cash flow', often defined as earnings before interest, taxation, depreciation and amortisation (EBITDA). EBITDA is essentially PBIT with depreciation and amortisation added back. As a result, EBITDA will usually be larger than PBIT, but it is a much better measure of a company's ability to service and repay its debt.
- If a company is struggling to achieve an acceptable level of interest cover (ie, above 1.5), this may indicate that it is too highly-geared (see Chapter 3, Section 4.2). If this is the case, the company needs to reduce its borrowings, perhaps by sweating its assets (ie, making them work harder) or even selling them.
- If the net interest payable figure is a higher percentage of average net debt for the year than would be expected, given the level of market interest rates, the company may have fixed its interest costs at a time when rates were high, or hasn't hedged its interest rate exposure.

1.2.2 Taxation

The taxation of companies in the UK is a highly complex subject. Every year, increasingly complicated legislation is added in the budget, and immediately afterwards, tax experts around the country must explain these new rules to their clients and train their staff in their application.

One huge drawback with this process is that each new set of rules seems to generate new loopholes, which has created a thriving tax avoidance industry (not tax evasion, which is illegal). Legitimate tax avoidance consumes a huge amount of time and effort, which is why very few companies actually pay the full rate of UK Corporation Tax (30% at present).

An example of this, taken from the Financial Review in the 2001 Annual Report and Accounts of Babcock International Group Plc, follows:

"Taxation

Excluding the net goodwill amortisation credit of £1.5 million and the non-operating exceptional loss of £6.2 million, the effective tax rate of 7.9% is lower than the standard UK rate of 30% due to the net effect of the utilisation of tax losses, surplus advanced corporation tax and short term timing differences not equalised through deferred tax. At 31 March 2001 the group had trading losses carried forward for tax purposes in excess of £70 million."

Tax losses can be carried forward for 6 years, and most taxable profits can be set off against them. Due to the complexity of the tax rules, taxable profit in the accounts is usually only a starting point for the computation of Corporation Tax due, and it is rarely possible for an outsider to make any connection between PBT and the tax charge in any particular year.

Most companies will include in the Notes a breakdown of the tax charge, but this is the tip of the iceberg.

1.2.3 Investing activities

Investing activities are important because they have a critical and often material effect on past, present and future financial performance.

Amounts spent on capital expenditure (Capex) are not debited to the P&L account but are added to fixed assets and subsequently depreciated. They can therefore comprise a significant cash outflow, and are only sheltered from tax to the extent that the depreciation charge is increased to reflect the new Capex invested during the year.

However, companies must invest in their business in order to be able to increase sales, increase efficiency and replace worn-out assets. Therefore, companies which are not investing at least as much as their depreciation charge, especially in asset-driven sectors such as manufacturing, are effectively running their business down, unless there are exceptional circumstances. If these circumstances exist they should be explained in the financial review, which usually includes from the Finance Director a reference to Capex .

1.2.4 Equity dividends paid

Equity dividends paid is the final deduction from the P&L account, and represents the amount to be paid to the shareholders out of post-tax profits.

Dividends are important, because shareholders and the financial markets generally are likely to value the shares according to the dividend income from them. Companies will therefore want to pay as much in dividends as they can, but dividend payments will reduce the amount of surplus cash retained in the company for future investment and expansion.

If a company is highly geared, lenders will take a dim view of a big dividend distribution, as it may adversely impact the company's ability to repay its debt in the future. In these circumstances, lenders may even try to restrict the amount of dividend paid by inserting some form of cash conservation covenant in a loan agreement, specifically referring to dividends.

The dividend payment is usually predicated on a per ordinary share basis, so the Financial Review in the Annual Report will announce that the final dividend will be "x" pence per share. It will also usually state whether the total dividend was greater or smaller than the previous year, and how many times the dividend was covered by EBITDA or some other calculation of earnings.

The final dividend is the figure used by analysts to calculate the investment performance of the shares, the company and the management, and these calculations are examined in more detail in Chapter 3.

1.3 MEASURES OF PROFIT

Given the structure of the P&L, showing as it does several sub-totals described as profit it is important to understand the ones that are used most frequently to assess performance and financial analysis. This is not always easy as, in the example P&L

from BOC shown in Section 1.1.3 above, there are no fewer than 8 sub-totals showing different profit figures, being:

Gross profit	1,491.0
ie, (sales turnover less the cost of producing the goods or services sold)	
Operating profit of subsidiary undertakings	499.6
ie, (gross profit less the cost of running the business and paying the workers ie, overhead and administration costs)	
Total operating profit including share of joint ventures and associates	556.2
ie, (operating profit plus any income from other businesses in which the company has an interest)	
Profit on ordinary activities before interest	568.7
Profit on ordinary activities before tax	457.2
Profit on ordinary activities after tax	353.5
ie, (PBT minus interest and tax)	
Profit for the financial year	326.4
ie, (calculated after adjusting for any minority interests, which are the profits of subsidiary companies that are not wholly owned by the parent company)	
Surplus for the financial year	156.2
ie, (the very last figure at the bottom of the P&L which shows the profits figure retained by the company, and added to the P&L reserve, after the payment of dividends)	

Following the release of FRS 3, items that were once branded Extraordinary Items should no longer appear in accounts. Extraordinary items were items that were so rare, and "outside the ordinary activities of a company... and are not expected to recur" that companies were permitted to take them below the line, ie, after the calculation of profit before tax. Anything of this nature should now appear as exceptional rather than extraordinary. Examples of the sorts of transactions that used to be considered extraordinary were:

- profits or losses from the sale of operations;
- reorganisation or restructuring costs; and
- profits or losses from the sale of fixed assets.

Quite why these were ever considered to be extraordinary is a mystery, unless it is connected to the increasingly volatile nature of a company's existence. What used to be extraordinary is now commonplace, but still exceptional, and therefore requiring separate disclosure on the face of the P&L account.

2. Balance Sheet

A balance sheet is a snapshot of all the company's assets and liabilities on the last day of its accounting period or financial year. It is the most frequently-used piece of information about a company's financial position, as it shows:

- what the company is worth in accounting terms (ie, whether its assets are greater than its liabilities);

- what its gearing percentage is (ie, how much debt it has compared to how much equity); and
- how liquid it is (ie, whether it can meet its liabilities as they fall due).

Many balance sheets are relatively easy to understand, as the headings in them are reasonably clear and evocative. However, there are many complications behind some of the headings, and although the heading itself may be self-explanatory, the methods used in arriving at the numbers are neither clear nor easy to understand.

Furthermore, many quoted or public companies are groups, consisting of a parent (often just a holding company) and a number of trading subsidiaries. In these cases, there will be two balance sheets in the report and accounts, one for the group (parent and subsidiaries combined) and one for the parent company. Although the word consolidation may sound self-explanatory, these two balance sheets may be quite different.

The assets of the parent company may consist almost entirely of the shares of the subsidiary trading companies, valued as per the accounting policies stated in the accounts. The balance sheet for the group will contain all of the fixed and working capital assets in use throughout the group.

The main elements of a balance sheet are as follows:

2.1 ASSETS

There are a number of different types of assets, which can broadly be categorised as fixed or current assets. Fixed assets are defined in the Companies Acts, and are, broadly speaking, the assets that a company uses on an ongoing basis in its business, and which facilitate its production of goods and or services, such as buildings, plant and machinery. Current assets are only held temporarily in the business, and are intended for consumption, liquidation or resale, and include such items as cash, raw materials and stock.

2.1.1 Fixed assets

There are broadly three types of fixed asset:

a) tangible fixed assets, which consist of land, buildings, plant and machinery;
b) intangible fixed assets, which consist of assets that are invisible, and which therefore have a value which is less easily determined; and
c) fixed asset investments, which consist of investments in subsidiaries, associated undertakings, properties, stocks, shares, bonds, etc, which the company intends to keep for more than one year.

Tangible Fixed Assets

As stated above, tangible fixed assets are used in the business to generate the production of goods or services, and are not held for consumption or resale.

Accounting for fixed assets is a minefield because of the many and various ways that such assets are acquired and held. For example, a company may have borrowed money to acquire an asset, which raises the question of whether the asset should be included in the balance sheet, as the company may not actually own the asset until it has paid off the debt.

However, even if all of a company's fixed assets were acquired with debt, it would be foolish not to recognise these assets in the accounts. Primarily, it should be recognised that there are assets being utilised in the business, and secondly, and perhaps more significantly, that there might be a material amount of debt to service and repay with the profits and cash flow from the business. The question is, how to recognise these assets and their matching liabilities, and as always, this has become immensely complicated.

Land and buildings are usually acquired with loans or mortgages, and plant and machinery with loans, hire purchase finance or leases. However, for accounting purposes, the only distinction between a mortgage, HP, loan or lease is whether the debt appears on the balance sheet or not. If it does not, then a company effectively has an asset producing profit for the business, but which does not appear on the balance sheet as an asset, nor does the finance used to acquire it show in the balance sheet as a liability.

The old accounting standard, SSAP 21, defined two different types of asset finance: finance leases and operating leases. SSAP 21 recognised that it was often very difficult to distinguish between these two structures, and indeed, an operating lease was defined in the standard as "a lease other than a finance lease."

This definition was not very helpful, so a rule of thumb was used, which was that if the Net Present Value (NPV) of the lease rentals was 90% or more of the original capital cost of the asset, then it was a finance lease. As such, the lease would have to be capitalised on the balance sheet as a liability and the underlying asset would also have to be recognised on the balance sheet.

This 90% rule was used purely for indication purposes, and was not a hard and fast element of the standard. A further distinction was that, with finance leases, the user (the lessee) would normally acquire or have acquired the asset at the end of the finance term, but with an operating lease, the asset would usually be returned to the lessor at the end of the lease.

However, various artificial finance lease structures were devised which, using the 90% rule of thumb, allowed companies to account for them as operating leases, giving them a source of off-balance sheet funding. With this type of funding, a company could theoretically acquire assets for use in their business without showing either the assets or the matching debt in the balance sheet, which would make them look much more productive and less highly-geared.

However, properly accounted for as a finance lease, the asset will be capitalised and depreciated over its useful life, or over the term of the lease, if shorter. The underlying lease will also be shown in the balance sheet. The NPV of the capital element will be shown under creditors, and the interest element taken through the P&L as the lease is extinguished.

For an operating lease, the useful life of the asset will usually be longer than the lease, so the user will only effectively be hiring the equipment, and the lease rentals will be charged to the P&L. At the end of the lease, the asset will return to the lessor. The lessor's profit in the transaction will come from having leased the asset for a primary period for a return higher than the carrying cost of acquiring it, plus the expected receipts from either an extension of the lease, a second lease or the disposal of the asset for its estimated residual value.

In both cases, the rental stream will normally be split between rentals due during the next year (creditors, in current liabilities) and rentals due beyond that (long-term creditors). The notes to the accounts will typically analyse leases or other asset financings for periods of less than one year, between two and five years, or six years and over.

Due to the creation of artificial lease structures and concerns over accurate disclosure of liabilities, SSAP 21 was augmented by FRS 5, which tries to use a substance over form approach in accounting for leases. Essentially, what the standard seeks to do is to establish whether a user has the risks and rewards associated with ownership, and if so, require the user to account both for the asset and for the underlying lease.

However, the standard is not prescriptive as to a number of issues concerning the value at which these assets and liabilities are accounted for, and the debate will doubtless continue for some time. The ASB is currently in consultation with the profession with a view to abolishing operating leases completely, so that in future, all leases and the underlying assets will be capitalised.

There is a further debate around the creation of off-balance sheet finance by raising debt through separate legal entities which do not meet the criteria for consolidation into the user's accounts. The collapsed US energy company Enron transferred large liabilities into a number of limited partnerships which were not consolidated into its accounts, leaving the company's balance sheet looking far healthier than it subsequently turned out to be.

Apart from investments and investment properties, fixed assets should always be depreciated. Fixed assets that do not depreciate (ie, do not wear out through usage) should be periodically re-valued, and such assets are investments and investment properties, which should be re-valued every year at market value. If properties other than investment properties (ie, the factories or offices which are used directly in the business) have increased in value, companies have the option of accounting for revaluation surpluses, but must in any event disclose material differences between the book value and the market value of all of their property assets.

Any gains or losses on property revaluations should be taken to revaluation reserves and not through the P&L, because they are unrealised, ie, there has been no cash impact. However, revaluation reserves are not distributable by way of dividend, so they are merely an adjustment to the company's net worth. This is to prevent unrealised gains being paid out as cash to shareholders, for the simple reason that should an asset's value fall in subsequent years, it is possible that negative net worth could be created in the balance sheet.

If properties have fallen in value, and that fall is deemed to be permanent, then revaluation deficits can be taken to the revaluation reserve, but only to the extent that the reserves already carry surpluses related to those assets which have suffered a deemed permanent diminution in value.

As always, these adjustments are subjective, and there is no requirement for revaluations to be carried out by qualified professionals.

Intangible fixed assets

For a non-accountant, the expression 'intangible fixed asset' might seem to be a contradiction, because if it is a fixed asset, how can it be intangible?

The Companies Acts defined some of them, and they include such items as brand names, goodwill, trademarks, development costs (capitalised R&D costs, for example), concessions, patents and licences.

In the case of trademarks, concessions, patents and licences, it is easy to see how these can be assets, as although they are only pieces of paper in the form of legal agreements, they are likely to generate income for the owner.

Capitalised R&D is more dubious, as there is no guarantee that the object of the R&D costs, whether capitalised or not, will generate income in the future. For example, a new drug may cost billions of dollars to research and develop, but may fail the all-important FDAA tests in the USA and never make it to market in order to recoup its development costs.

The really interesting intangibles are brand names and goodwill.

The best example of a brand name is Coca-Cola. A recent survey established the following as the world's Top 10 brands:

1. Coca-Cola;
2. Marlboro;
3. Pepsi;
4. Budweiser;
5. Campbell's;
6. Kellog's;
7. Pampers;
8. Benson & Hedges;
9. Camel; and
10. Danone.

At least 43 brands worldwide were estimated to be worth $1 billion or more. ('Reaching the Billion Dollar Mark' report by A C Nielson 2001).

A brand name is an asset. If, for example, a street trader is offering for sale an identical but unbranded cola product outside a supermarket that is selling Coca-Cola at three times the price, people are still more likely to purchase the supermarket's Cola. They do this because they recognise and trust the brand, and feel there is less risk in terms of quality and purity in buying that product, despite the difference in price, and despite the fact that the two drinks may well have exactly the same ingredients and cost the same to produce.

This means that the brand has a value to Coca-Cola, not just in terms of guaranteeing a larger volume of sales against other brands or products, but also because it is possible to sell it at a premium price. Value can be imputed to a brand, because, unless it is supported by extensive marketing and a commitment to the quality and longevity of the product, it will lose its value. Recent examples of damage to brands are legion:

- the benzine pollution of the Perrier source;
- the alleged use of child labour to produce Nike trainers;
- poor quality control at Jaguar in the 1970s and 1980s (somewhat rectified under Ford);
- Gerald Ratner's single-handed destruction of his family's jewellery chain by an ill-judged remark;
- the changing of old and valued consulting, postal services, truck, drinks and computer brand names into strange tongue-twisters (Accenture, Consignia, Navistar, Deagio, Unisys, etc).

The problem with brands is that it is impossible to say exactly and objectively what their value is, and accordingly standard setters have had problems doing so. This has led to widely varying values, valuation methodologies, depreciation policies and rates, and disclosure.

Goodwill represents a similar problem.

As stated above, the net asset figure in a balance sheet is not the real value of a company, and market capitalisation is a much better indicator. In the event of a takeover bid, if the purchaser paid more for the shares than the amount shown as the net asset value, the difference will be accounted for by the acquirer as goodwill. In other words, it is the difference between the 'fair value' (a much-loved accounting term) attributed to an investment in business or a subsidiary undertaking and the 'fair value' of the underlying net assets at the date of their acquisition.

Before FRS 10 was introduced for accounting periods ending after 1 January 1998, goodwill was always immediately written off against reserves as it was regarded as undesirable to carry it on the balance sheet. Since 1 January 1998 however, goodwill can be capitalised on the balance sheet as an intangible asset, along with things like brands, although depending on how easy they are to recognise, they may be carried separately in the accounts.

There is a proviso that goodwill must be written off over its useful life, and this concept would also apply to a brand, unless it was vigorously supported with marketing. This is an area where a lot of judgement can be applied, and it is not unknown for directors to take the view that their intangible assets have an infinite life.

However, it is much more common for these types of assets to be written off over fairly extended time periods, eg, between twenty and fifty years. Even if a brand name is heavily supported by investment, and thus remains highly valuable, and even if the value of an acquired subsidiary remains constantly above the value of its underlying net assets, it would still be prudent to write off such balances in any event, albeit relatively slowly.

Fixed asset investments

As stated above, fixed asset investments are assets which are retained for investment purposes, usually for periods longer than one year. Broadly speaking, investments fall into three categories: subsidiaries, associated undertakings and other investments (eg, properties, stocks, shares, bonds, marketable securities, etc). Such investments can be shown on the balance sheet as fixed assets or as current assets, should the company decide to sell them during its next financial year.

Subsidiaries

Subsidiaries are defined as being wholly-owned by the parent company, and all of their assets and liabilities will be consolidated into the parent company's accounts, usually appearing under fixed asset investments.

Associated undertakings

These are accounted for using a version of the equity method of accounting, which recognises the cost of the acquisition plus the group's share of any retained profits since the acquisition; in other words, the investor's share of the net worth of the investment.

Other investments

These are investments where the company owns less than 20% of the total equity of the target, and as such, does not need to consolidate the assets and the liabilities of the investment company in its accounts. Although consolidation of this investment is not required, an investment of 20% would be regarded as significant and the details of the investment should be disclosed. If an investment in another company represents more than 10% of that company's value or more than 10% of the investing company's net assets, disclosure is normally required.

Investments in quoted companies must be shown at cost, and any material variance from the market value must be disclosed. Investments in unlisted companies must be shown at cost or valuation.

2.1.2 Current assets

Current assets are the assets used in the business for conversion into goods and services for subsequent sale. There are some exceptions, such as consumables (eg, light bulbs for use in the factory or office, stationery, etc), work in progress (WIP) that relates to services on long-term contracts, and stock which is on consignment or reservation of title (ie, which is owned by one party but held by another party). FRS 5 is the relevant accounting standard for such items, and it decrees that such stock should be accounted for by the party that has the risks and rewards of ownership.

In order of liquidity (ie, how quickly they can be turned into cash), current assets are made up of cash, short-term investments, debtors, WIP, stock and loans.

Cash and short-term investments

These are reasonably self-explanatory. Investments must be shown on the balance sheet at the lower of cost and net realisable value, and investments should be analysed in the notes to the accounts.

Debtors

Debtors represent money owed to the business, net of any provision for bad and doubtful debts. A note to the accounts should analyse debtors into trade (ie, sales) and other debtors. It should also show amounts owed by group or participating undertakings to a parent company or investor, and prepayments and accrued income, which is money paid by the company in respect of goods or services not yet delivered and monies owed but not yet invoiced.

Debtors can be converted to cash by the process of debt collection, on which efficient companies spend a lot of time. Simple balance sheet analysis can show how many days' worth of sales proceeds remain uncollected, and these days can be compared to either the company's stated payments terms or against sector norms or best practice.

For example, the Electrocomponents Plc 2001 Accounts shown in Chapter 1 above, have turnover of £855.1 million and trade debtors of £147.3 million. The formula for the calculation of debtor days is:

$$\frac{\text{Trade debtors (£147.3m)}}{\text{Turnover (£855.1)}} \quad \text{x} \quad 365 \quad = \quad \text{62.9 days}$$

The rationale of this formula is that 17% of their annual sales remain unpaid for, and 17% of a year is 62 days.

To illustrate the importance of debt collection, imagine that Electrocomponents allowed their debtor days to extend to 90, so that it takes them 90 days to collect their debts. The debtors' figure in the accounts would increase to £210.4 million, which would mean that they had £63 million less cash. At today's interest rates, that could translate into more than £3 million per annum in lost interest, which would have increased net interest payable from £6.8 million to £9.8 million and reduced their pre-tax profit by nearly 3%.

WIP

Work in progress is stock that is making its way from raw materials to finished goods, plus all of the costs of the value added to it on the way, such as overheads and labour. It is merely a subdivision of the working capital assets of a company that are closer to cash than raw materials but not as close as finished goods or debtors (see below).

Stock

The Companies Acts require stocks to be analysed as either:

- raw materials and consumables;
- WIP;
- finished goods and goods for resale; or
- payments on account.

The accounting standard requires that stocks are classified as appropriate to the business, but usually the standard is not as prescriptive as the Companies Act. Stock valuations were covered in Section 1.1.2.

2.1.3 Current liabilities

Current liabilities are always netted against current assets in company reports and accounts, to show the net current assets/(liabilities) position. This is an attempt to represent the company's liquidity in as clear a way as possible. Fixed assets are not usually very liquid, and other liabilities, such as share capital or long-term debt are generally not repayable on demand. Therefore, net current liabilities give a good indicator of liquidity, ie, whether a company can meet its debts or liabilities as they fall due.

The major element of current liabilities is creditors, which is money owed within one year. These are required to be analysed as follows:

- bank loans and overdrafts;
- bills of exchange;
- payments on account;
- trade creditors;
- other creditors;
- corporation tax;
- other tax and social security;
- amounts owed to group undertakings (these will only appear on the parent's, or company balance sheet);
- amounts owed to associated undertakings;
- accrued expenses and deferred income; and
- proposed dividends.

Deferred income is that which has been received but no goods or services have yet been supplied. The prudence provision of the Acts requires that income should not be prematurely recognised in the P&L. Bills of exchange are still used, but so are many other new forms of short-term debt, so this list is not definitive and needs to be updated.

Although these creditors are not listed in any particular order, in the event of a winding up, there is a recognised order of priority, or preference for them. Generally speaking, the order is Corporation Tax, PAYE, VAT, secured bank debts and bondholders, then unsecured trade creditors and other creditors. Ordinary shareholders usually come last.

2.2 CREDITORS FALLING DUE AFTER ONE YEAR

This list is slightly shorter than the current liabilities, as some of them will always be payable within one year, such as tax, dividends and bills of exchange. The potential list of creditors falling due after one year is:

- bank loans;
- finance leases;
- payments on account;
- trade creditors;
- amounts owed to group undertakings (these will only appear on the parent's, or company balance sheet);
- amounts owed to associated undertakings;
- other creditors; and
- accrued expenses and deferred income.

Despite their nomenclature, the majority of the items in this section will be interest-bearing debt of some sort, and it will be very unusual for trade creditors, for example, to be payable in more than one year. In addition, most of this term debt will be secured by some kind of charge over the company's assets, either fixed and specific, or floating and general.

2.3 PROVISIONS FOR LIABILITIES AND CHARGES

Provisions were referred to in Section 1.1.4, which discussed the deduction of these charges from the P&L account. In the balance sheet there should be a breakdown of the overall position regarding these liabilities. They are held in the balance sheet as their timing or value cannot be accurately estimated, and during each financial year, the directors will make a charge or a write-back to the P&L as these liabilities either crystallise or disappear. As always, prudence and the need to present a true and fair view are the objectives in stating these balances and in retaining enough reserves in the company to meet them as they crystallise or fall due.

2.4 CAPITAL AND RESERVES

The above elements of the balance sheet comprise what are known as the net assets. This is a statement of the net assets and liabilities of the company, ie, the value of what it owns minus the value of what it owes.

According to the principal of the trial balance, for every £1 of net assets, there will be a £1 in capital and reserves. In other words, for every £1 invested in the company or retained by the company from past profits, there will be a matching asset valued at £1.

The money retained or invested will have been spent on something and must appear in the balance sheet, and the capital and reserves section is a statement of the accounting value of the shareholders' funds invested in the company, or a statement of how the net assets have been financed.

The main elements seen in balance sheet capital and reserves statements are:

Capital and Reserves	**Heading**
Called up share capital	The par value (ie, value at issue) of the issued share capital of the company.
Shares to be issued	eg, in respect of acquisitions.
Share premium account	The value received for the issue of ordinary shares over and above their par value.
Capital redemption reserve	Reserves held for the redemption of redeemable stock.
Merger reserve	Relating to shares issued in respect of acquisitions, against which goodwill arising on acquisitions made through a share premium account can be written off.
Revaluation reserve	Reserve relating to asset revaluations, which must be preserved separately for potential future devaluations. They can be transferred to the P&L reserve should the asset be sold and the revaluation profit crystallised.
Other reserves	Joint ventures' reserve, associates' reserve.
Profit & loss account	Retained earnings from prior years (ie, distributable reserves)
Equity Shareowners' funds	**Total**

Distributable reserves are those which can be paid out as dividends. Should a company not make a profit in any given year, it can still pay a dividend, but the dividend must be paid out of distributable reserves, and cannot be paid from any non-distributable reserves.

There are many different types of shares that can be issued by a company. Broadly speaking, they fall into four main categories:

- ordinary shares (the most common class of share, although within this class, there can be many different classes issued, having different voting rights, dividend entitlement or ranking in a winding-up);
- deferred shares (delayed or contingent dividends payable);
- redeemable shares (shares which the company must redeem at a predetermined time or value);
- preference shares (again, many different types of preference share can be issued, eg, cumulative, redeemable, participating or convertible, all of which confer varying rights on the holders).

It is also possible for companies to put long-term debt issues such as bonds, redeemable preference shares and mezzanine finance (convertible shares) in the bottom half of the balance sheet, as they are usually regarded as quasi-equity. Redeemable preference shares are often redeemable at a fixed, pre-determined date and value, and often have the right to a dividend whether or not the ordinary shareholders receive one. In many respects, they are more like debt than equity, in that the risks are similar. However, if any of these items incur interest charges, they should always be included as debt in any balance sheet gearing calculation.

To sum up, the balance sheet is a statement of the amount that has been invested in a company, or previously earned and retained and what current or long-term assets and liabilities that money has been spent on.

From this statement, it is possible to deduce the financial structure, strength, gearing and general financial well-being of the company, and whether it has sufficient funds to meet its debts as they fall due.

2.5 IMPACT OF CHANGES IN THE ISSUED SHARE CAPITAL (RIGHTS ISSUES, BONUS SHARES, ETC)

Companies are permitted to change their share structure to the extent set out in their memorandum and articles of association, and by company law.

Generally speaking, companies cannot reduce or cancel their issued share capital without permission, but they can buy it back. This tactic is sometimes used when companies have a lot of cash and cannot find any other use for it that will enhance shareholder value. This has a dual benefit for shareholders who choose to sell, by giving them back some cash and by enhancing the return on equity for the remaining shareholders in the future (ie, the company will produce the same level of earnings and dividend that it would have done without the buy-back, but on a smaller capital base).

Among the changes that might increase the issued share capital of a company (usually requiring the approval of the shareholders) are:

- new issues. If a company decides it needs more cash, it can sell some of its authorised but un-issued shares, perhaps to finance an acquisition. (For the acquisition, the company can either sell the shares in a new issue and pay cash for the acquisition, or just issue the new shares direct to the owners of the acquisition target in exchange for the target company's shares). The impact of a new issue will be to dilute the earnings and value of the existing shares in issue (ie, to reduce the value of the shares and dividend), unless the assets and income stream acquired are of a comparable pro-rata value to those of the acquirer;
- rights issues. If a company needs more cash, it can offer new shares to its existing shareholders on a pre-determined date, at a discount to the current market price. The impact is the same as for a new issue;
- bonus shares. A company can issue new shares to existing shareholders as an incentive, or perhaps to bolster the dividend (a scrip issue or dividend). The impact again is to dilute the value of existing shares; or
- a share split. If a company's share price has become too high for the shares to be marketable, it can split them. Individual shareholders typically prefer to own a large number of low-priced shares rather than a handful of very valuable shares.

Whenever a company issues new shares, particularly for an acquisition, analysts will look at the potential effect of any proposed capital change on share values and on earnings per share, because new or existing shareholders should be aware that the value of the shares going forward may be less than it had been in the past.

3. Cash Flow Statements

The whole subject of cash flow and how it is captured in reports and accounts is very complex and controversial.

People say “cash is king,” because without it, raw materials cannot be bought and suppliers and employees cannot be paid. Apparently profitable companies can go bankrupt because they run out of cash, but since profit necessarily involves selling output for more than it costs to deliver, how can this happen?

It is an illustration that, despite the best efforts of accounting standard setters over the years, it seems to be impossible to show clearly, in a set of accounts, how much free cash flow a company has generated.

Most measures of cash flow begin with accounting earnings, and as shown elsewhere, accounting earnings are highly subjective and can be prone to gloss or exaggeration. Under the current standards, cash flow statements have to show the cash outflows when loans are repaid, and the cash inflows when deposits mature, whereas any normal definition of cash would include loans and deposits. On examination, it is obvious where these loan and deposit movements are reconciled in the cash flow statement, but they do make them appear much more complicated than they need to be.

The importance of cash is most evident when companies are growing.

In order to grow, companies must acquire greater manufacturing or service delivery capacity, which involves acquiring additional staff, office or factory space, plant, machinery and raw materials. All of this absorbs cash, and when the final product or service is ready for sale, it has to be marketed, which involves more cost. All of these sales costs have to be financed from the point of supplier payment until the company's debtors pay it. This is more evident in manufacturing companies and less so in retail, but expansion does absorb cash.

Conversely, it is not always good for a company to generate cash. If it has been very successful in building its sales and growing its market share, but is not replacing worn-out assets, or investing in new processes or product lines, or watching what the competition is doing (perhaps developing a superior product), it might generate a handsome cash pile but could potentially end with no sales. It is surprising how quickly no sales can absorb a pile of cash.

The accounting standard requiring a cashflow statement in the accounts (FRS 1, replacing the source and application of funds statement) came about as a result of the fact that the P&L

account did not show whether a company was generating cash. As explained elsewhere, accounting profit does not equate to cash, and if a company is not generating sufficient cash to meet its liabilities as they fall due, whether it is profitable or not, it will fail.

The cashflow statement is supposedly very simple; it should show where the company has obtained its cash from and what it has spent it on. In that sense it is more like the P&L account than the balance sheet, as it shows a flow throughout the year rather than a snapshot at the end of it.

The cash flows must be analysed under the following headings:

- trading cash flow (funds flow from trading activities ie, selling goods and services for more than they cost to produce);
- interest and dividends (funds flows arising from investments and the servicing of finance);
- tax (funds flows from taxation); and
- purchase and sale of assets (confusingly called funds flows from investing activities).

These cash flows are summarised as being cash flows before financing, and show how funds have been acquired from or absorbed by these four areas of activity. The cash flow statement looks like a balance sheet, in that it states where the funds have been applied or acquired from. In other words, if the company has generated a cash surplus through the year, the surplus will have been placed on deposit, otherwise invested, or used to reduce debt or share capital. If the company had a cash shortfall, it will have issued more shares, reduced its investments or increased its borrowings.

The standard allows the cash flow statement to be prepared using the direct or the indirect method. The direct method is little-used, and simply states baldly and explicitly where the cash came from and what it has been spent on: ie, received from customers, paid to suppliers, paid to employees, other cash paid. This total must then be reconciled to the operating profit figure in order to show where the major differences lie.

The indirect method is the reverse; it starts with the operating profit and adds back non-cash items (mainly depreciation) to show whether cash has been generated by trading. It then analyses changes in working capital to show whether cash has been generated or absorbed during the year. This adjustment is necessary, because it is quite possible, as stated above, for stocks acquired and paid for in previous accounting periods to have been used in the production of goods sold in the current period. More new stock could also have been acquired and paid for than the amount of old stock turned into finished goods and sold in the current accounting period.

The example given in Chapter 1, Section 5.3 is interesting because what should be a relatively simple task (ie, to establish whether a company has generated cash or not during the year) is actually quite difficult. The eye is immediately drawn to the net cash inflow from operating activities, which is a whopping £142.2 million in cash, generated from £855.1 million in turnover.

From this £142.2 million went net interest payable (£6.7 million), taxation (£32.6 million), and capex and investment (£24.3 million), leaving £78.6 million in "free cash flow."

However, on further examination, the dividend of £54.3 million got paid from free cash flow, leaving £24.3 million as the net cash inflow "before use of liquid resources and financing. The notes to the accounts reveal that bank deposits decreased by £18.2 million, but that £3.8 million was received in consideration for new shares, leaving £46.3 million in cash sitting around. However, the final entry shows that bank debt was reduced by £46.6 million, leaving a cash <u>decrease</u> of £300,000 for the year.

Is this a good or a bad thing?

On balance, it is good, because £24.3 million in cash was generated through trading activity, interest and dividends, tax and the purchase and sale of assets. A further £3.8 million was received from the sale of shares, reducing the company's gearing. This cash, plus some bank deposits, was used to reduce debt by £46.6 million, which is a good thing.

To increase the confusion, a further reconciliation then occurs; net cash flow to movement in net debt. Starting with the decrease in cash of £300,000, the reduction in deposits of £18.2 million and the debt repayment of £46.6 million, (ie, the change in net debt relating to cash flows, net of currency translation differences) net debt decreased by £20.3 million during the year. The closing debt for the previous year was £95.8 million, so closing debt for 2001 was £75.5 million. Therefore net debt (ie, loans minus deposits) was only reduced by £20.3 million rather than the £46.6 million shown in the "use of liquid resources and financing" section.

Further detective work is then required to find the figure of £75.5 million, the net debt figure for 2001. To achieve this, one must look at current assets in the balance sheet to find:

	£m
Investments (also in note 21 as investments – current assets)	6.7
Cash at bank and in hand	10.6
	17.3

and Note 22, to find as part of creditors' amounts falling due within one year:

Bank overdrafts (unsecured)	(0.4)
Current instalment of loans (see Note 24)	(23.4)
	(23.8)

and Note 23, to find as part of creditors' amounts falling due after more than one year:

Loans repayable after more than one year (see Note 24)	(69.0)
	(75.5)

This is not a criticism of Electrocomponents Plc, whose accounts are, if anything, much simpler and clearer than many others. It is an observation that it always takes detective work to reconcile all of the different elements of the four financial statements before the picture becomes clear. This is particularly true when it comes to cash, which is vitally important, and should be the major feature in accounts. However, despite the requirement to show it clearly, it can still be obfuscated to the point where it is not clear whether or not companies are generating cash, and how much, but is always abundantly clear whether they are profitable in accounting terms.

The summary above is also interesting as, on the face of it, Electrocomponents is apparently arbitraging £17.3 million in deposits and cash in hand, and therefore paying 18% too much interest. However, it is likely that much of the surplus cash is in different territories to the loans and cannot therefore be used to repay them or set off against them.

This is the kind of calculation that is needed to make when deriving the gearing ratios, as set out in Chapter 3, Section 4.2. The current layout is confusing, because not only does it show transactions with shareholders (ie, raising of equity capital and payments of dividends), it also analyses how businesses manage their liquidity and financing, ie, how the cash gets moved around inside the company once it has been generated.

Cash outflows related to the purchase of liquid assets (investments) or repayment of debt, and inflows related to the sale of liquid assets or the drawing down of debt have nothing to do with financial performance. It would be far better therefore simply to analyse changes in net debt, which would be borrowings less cash investments.

Many analysts therefore restate cash flows in their own formats, separating operating from financing cash flows. They also try to establish whether a company is really generating cash (it is far more difficult to create cash than to create profit), whether there are specific reasons why it is or isn't, and whether that cash flow is sustainable.

Key factors are things like financial profile (gearing, fixed and working capital asset weighting, etc), markets and business environment, whether the company is growing or not, whether it is replacing its fixed assets, whether it is paying tax, interest and dividends and whether there have been any acquisitions.

A simplified cash flow analysis would look like this:

Item	£	Description
❑ Operating profit ❑ Depreciation ❑ Other non-cash items		Operating profit + interest received Profits on disposal, etc
Operating cash flow (A)		
❑ Decrease/(increase) in stock ❑ Decrease/(increase) in debtors ❑ Decrease/(increase) in creditors		Working capital changes, which must be sustainable given the companies trading position.
Working capital flow (B)		**Often negative for growing businesses**
Operational cash flow (A+B) ❑ Interest received/(paid) ❑ Net capex ❑ Tax received/(paid) ❑ Dividends received/ (paid)		
Free cash flow		**Defined as cash available to repay debt**
Funded by: ❑ long- and short-term debt ❑ equity ❑ investments ❑ cash ❑ acquisitions ❑ others		This section should show where free cash outflows were financed from or inflows were disbursed or invested. Acquisitions are included here as they are discretionary.

When this type of analysis has been carried out, it is easy to see whether operational cash flow is positive, where that cash flow came from, whether interest and dividends payments are adequately covered by profit and free cash flow, and whether capex is at least equal to depreciation. Over a period of years, the trends in cash flow can also be analysed, to monitor whether it is sustainable or whether there are large variations year on year.

The difficulty with accounting for cash is that the starting point for calculating cash flow is always operating profit (which can be affected by subjective opinions), plus or minus the adjustments to sales revenues and costs that are permissible under accounting standards. Simply adding back the obvious non-cash items (depreciation and amortisation) to this figure will not produce an accurate cash flow, unless all of the other adjustments to revenues and costs are reversed out too, which will represent a huge additional accounting and disclosure burden.

The key importance of cash to a business, whether growing or shrinking, and the seeming difficulty with demonstrating clearly in the report and accounts whether or not companies are generating it, represents a serious weakness at present, but there is a powerful ongoing debate on the subject, and FRS 1 and FRED 10 will not be the last words on the subject.

There can always be timing differences between profit and cash which mean that a company might show good profits whilst having less positive cashflow or even cash outflows. Examples are:

- companies with major recurring and increasing capex (where depreciation expense will never, as a result, catch up with cash spend); and
- companies that are growing very rapidly and have a resulting major recurring increase in working capital requirements (receivables plus stock less payables).

However, in the long-term, real profits have to equal real cash (prior to payments to shareholders and to strategic transactions such as acquisitions) because, by definition, a real profit means that revenues (cash in) are greater than expenses (cash out).

4. Statement of Recognised Gains and Losses

This primary statement was introduced under FRS 3 (Reporting Financial Performance). It shows gains and losses made by a company which have not been shown in the P&L as they are unrealised, and have therefore been taken straight to reserves. Any movements in reserves are shown elsewhere in the reports and accounts, but unrealised gains and losses could previously have accounted for movements in reserves that were not shown anywhere else in the primary statements, and merely appeared in the notes.

The addition of this primary statement precluded the necessity to drill down through the notes to the accounts in order to reconcile movements in reserves with the other primary statements. With the addition of this statement, plus the detail in the P&L, the casual reader should be able to see all of the gains and losses made by a company during the financial period.

The statement summarises all recognised gains and losses, ie, those included in the accounts, but not necessarily realised. Unrealised gains and losses could include changes in the market value of assets or investments (which are unrealised because those assets or investments have not been sold, and therefore the changes in value have not been crystallised) or changes in the translation value of foreign currency denominated assets and liabilities. Taking the 2001 accounts for Electrocomponents again:

Consolidated statement of total recognised gains and losses For the year ended 31 March 2001		
	2001 £m	2000 £m
Profit for the financial year	**72.6**	**73.9**
Translation differences	**24.4**	**(6.0)**
Total recognised gains and losses relating to the year	**97.0**	**67.9**
All profits and losses are stated at historical cost. The statement of movement on Group reserves is at Note 31. The notes on pages 45 to 60 form part of these accounts.		

At the risk of causing confusion, these are the total recognised gains and losses relating to the year, not the movements in shareholders' funds, which in Electrocomponents' accounts are reconciled at Note 31. Some of the same numbers will appear in that reconciliation, such as the translation difference and the retained profit for the year, but other items could cause shareholders' funds to change, such as changes in share capital or movements in goodwill.

5. Group Accounts

Many quoted company accounts have two balance sheets, one entitled 'Group' and one entitled 'Company.' To add to the potential confusion created by the existence of two balance sheets, they are usually completely different to each other.

The explanation is relatively simple. The 'Company' balance sheet refers to the parent or holding company of the group, and the 'Group' balance sheet is the consolidated balance sheet.

It is often the case that the parent has very little in its balance sheet apart from large liabilities to the shareholders or lenders, and the large asset represented by the value of its investment in the trading companies. The parent is usually a non-trading legal entity that raises the share capital and loan finance to acquire the trading companies. The trading subsidiaries, or 'Undertakings' as they are usually referred to in the accounts are the legal entities that acquire premises, hire workers, purchase plant, machinery and raw materials, and carry out the production, marketing, sales and distribution activities of the group.

In addition to the above distinction, there is a requirement to consolidate the activities of the group in the accounts so that any assets, liabilities, cash flow and profits that originate from companies not wholly-owned by the parent can be split out.

When parent companies control other companies (control as defined in the Companies Acts, which can mean the ability to influence the running of the other company even if the controlling company does not own the majority of the shares), it must show the sales, cost of sales, assets and liabilities in its consolidated accounts, but must then show in the P&L that element of the consolidated profits that do not belong to the parent company.

There is an example of a deduction for minority interests in the BOC P&L shown in Section 1.1.3. In a simpler example, if Company A owns 75% of Company B, their P&Ls would look like this:

	Company A	Company B	Consolidated
	£m	£m	£m
Turnover	700	300	1,000
Cost of sales	(500)	(190)	(690)
Gross profit	200	110	310
Net operating expenses	(150)	(80)	(230)
Profit before tax	**50**	**30**	**80**
Tax on profit on ordinary activities	(15)	(10)	(25)
Profit on ordinary activities after tax	**35**	**20**	**55**
Minority interests			(5)
Profit for the financial year	35	20	50
Dividends – equity	(25)		(25)
Surplus for the financial year	10	20	25

The deduction for minority interests represents the proportion of the after-tax profit attributable to the minority shareholders of the other company. However, you will never see this calculation in the accounts as the Companies Act does not require the disclosure of the parent company's P&L account.

The other elements you might see in a parent company's balance sheet are amounts owed to/ receivable from group undertakings (inter-company loans within the group of wholly-owned companies) or amounts owed to/ receivable from associated undertakings (inter-company loans within the group of controlled and consolidated companies).

6. Summary

It is reasonably clear from this section that the primary statements and notes to the accounts of public companies are vastly complicated to construct, and are often very difficult even for qualified and experienced readers to understand. It is also evident from the number of companies that fail, or that prove on takeover or flotation to be worth a lot less than was supposed, and the number of professional investors and financial institutions that lose money on investments, that many professionals get it wrong. It is necessary to ask the question "Why are they so complicated?"

The sorts of considerations that have gone into the accounting standards and that therefore go into constructing a set of accounts are considered elsewhere in this book. Whilst these considerations may seem logical and reasonable to professional accountants, stock analysts, fund managers and auditors, the lay reader is going to find it very difficult to follow a set of accounts, and often even harder to draw any sensible conclusions from them. Nonetheless, they are obliged to try to do this in order to make important investment or lending decisions.

The problem appears to be that that reports and accounts are not really intended for lay readers, which therefore effectively excludes these readers from a full understanding of the financial affairs of public companies. Unfortunately, any attempt to simplify reports and accounts will almost certainly lead to less information, less disclosure and more concealment and obfuscation, thereby providing less assurance for analysts and investors.

3

ANALYSIS, INTERPRETATION AND PERFORMANCE MEASUREMENT

1. Introduction

As reports and accounts are such complex documents, the task of analysing and interpreting them is fraught with difficulty.

Reports and accounts contain a snapshot of the financial position at the end of the year (the balance sheet) and a series of flow statements that purport to show how much accounting profit has been made (the P&L), how much cash has been generated (the cash flow) and what the overall gains and losses for the year have been, reconciled to movements in shareholders' funds (the STRGL). It should therefore be possible to reconcile the three flow statements with the difference in shareholders' funds from one balance sheet to the next.

Once that task has been achieved, there are the numerous more difficult tasks of deciding whether that company is doing well or badly, given the state of its markets, how its competition is doing and whether more income could be earned from the money if it was invested elsewhere. In other words, how is the company performing?

Should investors leave their money invested in this company or move it to another? Is the management doing a good job of competing in its markets, maintaining market share, staying competitive on price and quality, keeping customers happy? Are they maintaining or improving profit margins? Are they keeping overheads under control? Are their competitors doing better, staying leaner, gaining market share, achieving higher profit margins?

A study of a company's reports and accounts can answer some of these questions, but the key thing to note is that they are not really designed for this purpose, and need a lot more analysis before they yield this kind of information.

They are primarily designed by the company's financial managers to give shareholders information as to how their investment is performing. As such, some information about shareholder ratios is provided, such as:

- earnings per share (EPS - profit after tax divided by the number of ordinary shares in issue); and
- price/earnings ratio (P/E ratio - share price divided by EPS).

These two pieces of information are often prominently presented in the chairman's, chief executive's or finance director's review, provided they are attractive numbers.

Apart from the statutory and regulatory requirements, directors have a fairly free rein in respect of what goes into the accounts for marketing purposes, to attract new shareholders or investors. As a result, they are often glossy, colourful, upbeat and of very good quality in terms of paper weight and reproduction (unless the company is doing badly).

If the company is doing well, it is common to see EPS and P/E figures being quoted, and compared to previous years, but they are usually quoted in absolute terms, not relative to the competition. You may see an attempt to compare them with the sector, but the sector is fairly amorphous, and can contain companies with other activities or a different mix of activities, differing capital structures, different cost bases, etc, which will make comparisons very specious.

This is the main problem with the analysis of accounts. Not only is it very difficult to obtain or derive meaningful comparisons with other companies, it is often impossible to achieve this with other companies ostensibly operating in the same sector. Most books, articles or training courses that use financial ratio analysis emphasise their limitations, but then admit they are using them in the absence of anything better.

For the purposes of these calculations, ratios can be divided into sub-sets, each meeting the requirements of different types of stakeholders and each saying something about how the company is run and how it is performing. Investors want to see the value of their investment growing and yielding good income. Managers want to see profits growing so that their bonuses and share options get paid, the share price stays high and they retain their independence. Lenders want to see cash being generated so that their loans can be serviced and repaid.

All of these requirements are reasonably congruent, differing only in degree. For example, in good years, managers may suppress profits to the minimum level to ensure that their bonuses are paid, thus being able to release sufficient stored-up profit in the bad years to trigger their bonuses again. They may also want to smooth profit growth so that expectations are not raised by spectacular performance in good years, possibly resulting in their censure or dismissal when these results are not repeated in the bad years. However, they must balance this smoothing with the need to keep the share price up.

It is therefore conventional to relate certain performance measures to certain stakeholder groups:

- for managers, profitability, return on capital;
- for shareholders, return on equity, earnings per share, price/earnings ratio; and

- for lenders, liquidity, solvency, gearing, interest cover, dividend cover.

Although it is accepted that financial analysis can only ever be as good as the data being examined, providing there is a sound framework for analysis of ratio and cash flows, and that other analysts have used broadly the same measures, it is possible to get some value from it, with caveats. Convention in these matters has never been codified, but is studied and taught widely and a lot of information is available on the subject. Following this type of comparable analysis, benchmarks can be established.

2. Management Performance Measures

2.1 INTRODUCTION

Managers are the individuals entrusted by the shareholders with the stewardship of their investment. Executive directors and other board members are elected by the shareholders, and are accountable directly to them. These directors recruit and retain the best managers they can, and are responsible for the performance of all the managers reporting to them, down through the organisation. There is a whole science of human resource and organisational development, but at its simplest, the elected directors are responsible to the shareholders for the performance of the company and the managers are responsible to the directors. Their concerns and attitudes will differ accordingly.

Although the shareholders will ultimately look at the performance of their investment, they must also look at the performance of the company itself. It is possible that a company can be performing well, but for reasons outside its control, the shares are doing badly, and vice versa. The following ratios can be used to judge the company's management and their use of the company's assets to generate a return.

2.2 RETURN ON CAPITAL EMPLOYED (ROCE)/ RETURN ON ASSETS (ROA)

This is one of the most basic performance ratios, and shows the return on the capital and assets employed in the business (ie, profitability), calculated as follows:

$$\frac{\text{Profit before long-term interest and tax}}{\text{Capital employed}} = \text{ROCE}$$

and

$$\frac{\text{Profit before long-term interest and tax}}{\text{Assets}} = \text{ROA}$$

These ratios give an indication of whether the company's management is doing a good job in terms of applying the funding and assets provided to best use. They do not tell shareholders how their investments are doing because the assets and capital employed in the business are accounting figures unrelated to the market capitalisation, which is the actual value of the company on the stock market.

It would be helpful if the above two ratios were easily found in reports and accounts, but they are not.

For a genuine indication of performance, long-term loans are usually included in capital employed, as they can be a major element in its financing. If a balance sheet is highly geared, or leveraged (see Section 4.2) and was making a high return, it would show a very high ROCE, whereas the true figure, including debt in capital employed, could be much lower.

Using long-term debt in capital employed allows a comparison between companies with differing capital structures, although debt and equity have quite different costs associated with them and will distort performance at some level. Debt is usually more expensive than equity (ie, loan interest costs more than dividends) and there is no option as to whether it is paid or not. If a company performs worse than its competition as a result of having a highly geared balance sheet, it may consider some form of share issue to try to reduce its cost of capital.

PBIT is also not commonly found as a discrete value on P&L statements, and is usually described as profit before interest, as tax is deducted from the P&L after interest. However, to obtain a valid ROCE, the interest on the long-term loans described in the previous paragraph should be added back, after the interest on working capital debt has been deducted. This will require some detective work along the lines described in Chapter 2, Section 3 above. However, it is not always the case that long-term interest is analysed separately and this calculation may be difficult to perform.

As already stated, profits are the result of subjective decisions and the method of calculating them can vary between companies. A study of accounting policies in the notes to the accounts will confirm whether the profits of any two companies are really comparable. There is also the issue of whether such things as provisions, or other potentially non-recurring or non-trading items, should be eliminated from the PBIT figure, again to make the comparison valid, as these items can be used to smooth profits between years.

This phenomenon demonstrates why ratios should be looked at in context and why trends are more important than snapshots.

2.3 PROFIT MARGIN

Profit margin is the operating profit expressed as a percentage of annual sales.

Operating profit is used here because it does not include non-trading or non-recurring elements and is a clearer indicator of the performance of the underlying business. As annual sales turnover and operating profit are clearly defined in the report and accounts, this is an easier ratio to derive than most of the others. This makes trend analysis, comparison against the competition, comparison with the sector and comparison with other sectors easier to achieve.

As operating profit relates to the basics of the business, it is also a clear indicator of how well the company is managing its markets, sales and costs, especially working capital costs.

Typical analysis examines gross and operating margins.

Gross margin is calculated as follows:

$$\frac{\text{Gross profit}}{\text{Turnover (sales)}} \quad \text{x} \quad 100$$

and operating margin is calculated as follows:

$$\frac{\text{PBIT}}{\text{Turnover (sales)}} \quad \text{x} \quad 100$$

3. Investment Performance Measures

Investors have a different set of priorities and concerns from management.

They are concerned with growing and maximising their return, consistent with their views on risk. Their concern is to see growth in the value of their shares (and therefore in the company's market capitalisation) plus dividends received, less new capital injected into the company. This is the shareholders' perspective on performance measurement.

Direct investment in equities is increasingly rare, as individual investors look to spread their risk and diversify their portfolios. They have funds tied up in equities, probably through life assurance policies, pension funds, ISAs, etc. Many choose to hold their surplus investments in unit trusts or some other vehicle that holds and manages direct investments on their behalf.

Increasingly it is professional investors, or fund managers, who are making direct equity investments, rather than individuals. Given the complexity of digging through reports and accounts, it is no wonder that only professionals can make enough sense of them to make informed investment decisions.

Whether they are individuals or fund managers, investors are concerned with several key performance ratios; return on equity (ROE) and price/earnings ratio (P/E). They will also look at earnings per share (EPS), which is published in the report and accounts, and the level of reported dividend per share.

Of equal importance is trend. Analysts will always look for discernible positive trends, which is why accountants so often yield to the temptation to smooth profits by storing value in the balance sheet. The problem with doing this is that investors can become convinced that a company is doing well, when in actual fact it is doing badly, but management is actually releasing profits stored from previous years.

Releasing value from the balance sheet can conceal weaknesses, but it is very difficult to persuade managers not to do it. It is also relevant that this stored profit could have been distributed to shareholders in previous years, so they will have suffered a cashflow disadvantage, in addition to being fooled by the subsequent release of this value, disguised as current year profit.

Other growth indicators that should be analysed relate to whether the growth comes from acquisition or from genuine organic growth of the business, and if organic, which particular parts of the business or parts of the world are providing that growth. Growth is also not necessarily always positive, because it can demand investment in fixed and working capital assets; heavy investment in a growth area could backfire if the growth is a blip rather than something sustainable.

3.1 RETURN ON EQUITY (ROE)

ROE shows the overall return on shareholders funds, the so-called net worth of the company. It is calculated as follows:

$$\frac{\text{Profit attributable to ordinary shareholders}}{\text{Shareholders' funds}} \quad \text{x} \quad 100$$

This ratio shows the performance of the company in providing a return to shareholders based on funds attributable to them. This is of course just the accounting value of shareholder funds, and not the value of the shareholders' investment, which is the market capitalisation of the company. Profit is also just an accounting measure, so it is a ratio entirely dependent on accounting input and construct.

Whilst this figure is interesting to shareholders, the trend of this return and the rates of returns achieved by the company's competitors or other sectors of the market are more interesting. Based on this ratio, investors can form an opinion as to how the company is performing, but the ratio carries a health warning as material changes in capital and reserves will have a considerable impact on it, particularly if those changes are near the end of the year.

For example, if there is a large write-off of goodwill towards or at the end of the year, a low profit figure might look better against the lower figure for capital and reserves that was showing at the end of the year, rather than the figure that was available throughout the year.

3.2 EARNINGS PER SHARE (EPS)

EPS is calculated as follows:

$$\frac{\text{Profit attributable to ordinary shareholders}}{\text{Number of ordinary shares in issue}} \quad \text{x} \quad \text{EPS}$$

This shows how much money the company has made that is attributable to ordinary shareholders, divided by the number of ordinary shares in issue. This does not mean that the ordinary shareholders will receive this sum in dividends; it is merely the amount that is attributable to them. Any profit not distributed as dividend will be retained in the company, theoretically increasing its capital value, which along with dividends, is the other source of income to shareholders.

Each year the company must decide how much of its retained earnings it will distribute as dividend. If it pays out too much, it could raise expectations for the future, increase the value of the shares disproportionately and leave the company short of cash.

Again, profit attributable to ordinary shareholders is not explicitly shown on every P&L account, but whatever it is called, (profit/(loss) for the year, profit on ordinary activities after taxation, etc) it is the last figure in the P&L before the dividend is deducted.

SSAP 3 is the accounting standard that dictates how EPS should be calculated and disclosed. In addition to the basic method set out above, there are other adjustments that need to be made to account for the tax effect of paying dividends (if material) and the effect on EPS of the exercise of all outstanding share options.

3.3 DIVIDEND PER SHARE AND DIVIDEND COVER

Dividend per share is simply the total declared ordinary dividend divided by the number of ordinary shares in issue, which is often explicitly disclosed in the accounts. Companies are expected to maintain or increase this figure every year, and any declaration that the dividend payment is to be reduced often causes the share price to fall, even though the company may be just as strong and profitable as before. This illustrates again the fact that the accounting profit and net worth are unrelated to the share price.

Dividend cover is simply the calculation of the number of times that the declared dividend could be paid out of that year's profit. This can be done either using the gross figures or the individual figures:

$$\frac{\text{Profit attributable to Ordinary Shareholders}}{\text{Declared dividend}} \quad \text{or} \quad \frac{\text{EPS}}{\text{Dividend per share}}$$

Whilst paying a healthy dividend will be applauded by shareholders (it is after all why they are investing) retaining distributable profit in a company is a prudent move by the management. This retained cash could reduce borrowing costs and insulate them from some of the effects of bad times.

Lenders want to see shareholders rewarded, but do not want to see too much paid in dividends while a heavily geared company still has lots of senior debt outstanding. Indeed, some loan documents contain covenants regarding the maximum permitted dividend payouts during senior debt repayment periods.

3.4 PRICE/EARNINGS RATIO (P/E RATIO)

The above ratios are all accounting ratios in that they look at book values rather than market values. As already stated, there is often a very large gap between these two, as companies' shares usually trade at either a discount or a premium to net worth.

The P/E ratio looks at company profitability as a function of the market share price, and is calculated as follows:

$$\frac{\text{Today's middle share price}}{\text{EPS}}$$

The middle price is midway between the buy and the sell prices quoted by dealers.

This ratio is commonly published in the Financial Times or on the various company or market news services (eg, Reuters, Bloomberg, etc), but often has to be calculated from adjusted figures. As stated above, SSAP 3 sets out the three options as to how this figure should be calculated.

The news services will recalculate the figure according to the net basis (ignoring the impact of tax) then adjust for gains or losses on the sale of assets or subsidiaries and for exceptional asset write-downs if the fall in value is deemed by the company to be permanent. This latter adjustment will not be made if the assets are going to be sold, in which case, as the gains or losses on those assets will shortly be realised in the accounts, they are left in the calculation. Once these adjustments have been made, all of the P/E ratios published by these services will have become comparable.

The primary use of this ratio is its predictive value. A low P/E ratio may be indicative of a company that pays out large dividends, but does not retain profits or grow in value. It could also indicate that the share price is low because there is an expectation that earnings will fall. A high P/E ratio will not give the investor a good dividend return, but may repay them with capital growth, because either the company retains profits and grows or there is an expectation that it will become more profitable and the dividend will grow in the future.

3.5 DIVIDEND YIELD

Dividend yield is also shown in market news services, and simply restates the dividend as a percentage, so that it can be compared to other forms of investment. It is calculated as follows:

$$\frac{\text{Dividend per share}}{\text{Today's middle share price}}$$

Comparing dividend yield with other forms of investment is not a simple matter of yield; investors also have to factor in the inherent risks in holding shares directly as opposed to placing deposits with banks or building societies, for example. Generally speaking, over the long term, equities produce better returns, because the investor receives a dividend and also benefits from capital growth. It is a matter of comparing risk and potential reward over time.

4. Financial Structure and Efficiency

Profitability and investment performance ratios were examined above, and it was noted that these are derived from accounting numbers, which are the result of subjective decisions from the management of a company. The directors, elected and paid by the shareholders, are reporting to them how well they have performed in providing a return on their investment.

It has also been stated throughout this book that, regardless of whether it is profitable, a company can still fail due to a lack of cash or liquidity. In other words, it can become insolvent, meaning it is unable to pay its debts or meet its liabilities as they fall due for payment.

Arguably, the following financial performance measures are the critical ones, because they can give an early indication of the likelihood of problems with liquidity. These are also the checks that lenders or bond investors will make before advancing any money to the company.

An investor gives the company money in exchange for a share of its profits and assets. The value of its investment can rise, fall or be lost forever. It could receive a healthy, adequate or inadequate dividend, or no dividend at all. Should the value of its investment be lost completely, that is all that can be lost, and creditors cannot go to an investor and ask for any more money. Nor can shareholders go to a public company with their share certificate in hand and ask for their money back. If shareholders want to dispose of their investment, they must find buyers for the shares.

Lenders and bondholders have a different perspective to investors. They are advancing money to a company, usually for a predetermined period, following which they expect to get their money back. During the period of the advance, they will receive a set-up fee at the beginning of the advance and regular interest payments thereafter, usually at higher rates than dividend payments.

Only in the case of overdrafts can the lender demand repayment of the advance, but companies will rarely be dependent on these for their entire financing and will always try to obtain secure term funding to reduce refinancing risk, which is the risk that they will find themselves short of loan facilities.

Lenders will often take security for loan advances, usually in the form of a legal charge over the borrower's assets. They will also have some form of agreement to cover the loan, which will include financial covenants to protect the lender in the event of a default.

Financial covenants are financial performance hurdles over which the company must jump, either at pre-determined dates (usually accounting period ends) or at all times. They usually relate to profits, balance sheet gearing and cash flow, and require the company to meet certain ratios in each category. Examples are given at each stage below.

Should the borrower fail to meet these covenant requirements (ie, be in default of the terms of the agreement) the lender can quote the relevant section of the loan agreement and demand that the relevant conditions be met. These can range from a simple renegotiation of the agreement, often accompanied by an increase in fees and margins, to a demand for full and immediate repayment of the loan and all outstanding interest. If this latter eventuality occurs, the company is usually not in a position to find the cash from other lenders, and either has to ask the shareholders for more money or put itself up for sale.

If the shareholders have to provide more money, arguably for shares that will have fallen in value as a result of the share call, the value of their investment is said to have been diluted. In other words, although they have invested more money, the proportion of the company that they own has not risen, and indeed as stated above, the value of the overall investment may have fallen. If a white knight comes to the rescue, the company may lose its independence, the managers might lose their jobs and the shareholders could suffer an even greater dilution of their investment.

Should the company fail, secured lenders rank above ordinary shareholders for any distribution and will rarely lose their entire loan. They will also try to achieve a surplus margin of asset value over their loan, known as the loan-to-value ratio, so that they can recoup more from the sale of these assets than the outstanding loan balance.

If an asset has been repossessed because the borrower has defaulted on the loan, the lender may have to conduct a forced sale of the asset into a depressed market (known colloquially as a fire-sale) to get rid of it. What this means is that the lender is not a willing seller in that they have to sell the asset in order to remove the bad loan from their books.

Furthermore, if there has been a downturn in the economy (and these do cause more borrowers to default on their loans) many people may be trying to sell similar assets into an already depressed market. In a situation where an unwilling seller is trying to sell into a buyer's market, and having to do it as soon as possible, it can be difficult to achieve full value for the asset. However, if the lender has achieved a reasonable margin of value over loan, the chances are that, even in the fire sale situation, the asset will still yield sufficient proceeds to repay the debt.

On the face of it, lenders do rather better than investors in that their interest receipts are always larger than dividends, and they rank above shareholders in a liquidation. However, lenders do not share in any capital gain in the value of the company. They will also only lend money when they can see there is a very good chance that their loan will get serviced and repaid from cashflow, rather than from having to repossess charged assets and sell them.

Therefore, the risk and reward ratio is entirely different for lenders and investors, which is why lenders look at accounts in an entirely different way. Shareholders will look at things like capital growth or dividend payment history, whilst lenders will look at cashflow, asset values and security.

4.1 LIQUIDITY/SOLVENCY

It is illegal for company directors to allow a company to continue trading when it is insolvent. However, as with all things to do with accountancy, the definition of insolvency is open to differing interpretations. As was seen in 2001, the DTI put Railtrack Plc into administration, stating that it was insolvent and "plummeting toward a financial abyss." The shareholders and management took the completely opposite view, with the shareholders resorting to legal action to try to get their investment back.

Solvency usually means:

- positive net current assets (ie, assets greater than liabilities); and
- ability to meet debts or other liabilities as they fall due.

As the former depends on things like asset values (stocks, debtors, WIP, brand names, goodwill, properties, investments, etc) the levels of provisions for bad and doubtful debts and other permanent diminutions of value, it can be seen that management opinions will largely decide whether the company is solvent by that measure.

Debts and other liabilities are less easy to disguise as they will be things like trade creditors, other creditors (eg, tax, PAYE, VAT, etc) and loans or overdrafts, which will be in the accounts at their face value. There is some scope to determine that some liabilities are contingent rather than real but generally, they are more easily valued than assets.

However, the ability of the company to pay them is usually judged by the value of the assets that can be liquidated or utilised to pay them, and these, of course, can be obfuscated, as stated above. Whether or not these assets can be liquidated to meet liabilities is one of the reasons why liquidity ratios are assessed at two levels: current and quick liquidity.

Summarising the current assets in the Electrocomponents balance sheet above as follows:

Electrocomponents Plc CONSOLIDATED BALANCE SHEET	**£m**
Current Assets	
Stocks	165.3
Debtors	168.9
Investments	6.7
Cash at bank and in hand	10.6
	351.5
Creditors: amounts falling due within one year	(202.1)
Net current assets	149.4

The company therefore meets one criterion of solvency: it has positive net current assets. The other criterion needs further examination.

On the face of it, Electrocomponents Plc has almost £1.74 in current assets for every £1 owed in liabilities falling due within one year, which represents a current liquidity ratio of 1.74: 1 (£351.5m divided by £202.1m).

However, whilst this may reasonably be said to imply that the company can meet its debts as they fall due, as always, further examination is required. Apparently the company only has £10.6 million in cash, yet owes £202.1 million. How does one judge whether they would actually be able to meet these liabilities? The answer is a question. Would anyone among us be able to pay from their available cash resources if all of their creditors (mortgage, credit cards, overdrafts, utility bills, rent, etc) requested their money at the same time?

To answer this question, the nature of the assets and liabilities must be examined. Taking the assets first:

	£m
Stocks	165.3

Note 19 to the accounts states that stock comprises:

	£m
Raw materials and consumables	2.6
Work in progress	3.2
Finished goods and goods for resale	159.3
Total:	165.3

Raw materials and consumables and work in progress are not usually included in the quick liquidity or solvency ratios, as they are reckoned to be too far in time from liquidation. In other words, more time and more money must be spent on them before they can be sold for cash. Electrocomponents Plc has very liquid stocks, with more than 96% of its value being finished and ready for resale, and which would be included in the quick ratio.

Whilst this appears to be a good situation, it is not healthy if a company has too much money tied up in a level of stock that is high in absolute terms and high relative to competitors or rising year-on-year. Stock costs money to acquire and to hold, may cost interest on money borrowed to hold it, will cost in terms of storage and handling, and may also cost if it deteriorates whilst being held. This is a particularly important consideration if stocks are perishable, eg, fresh food.

To find out whether stocks are high in absolute terms, the stock turn and stock days figures should be examined. The latter figure is the time period over which the entire value of stocks (or finished goods) is sold. It needs attention because the finished goods figure is so high. It is calculated as follows:

$$\frac{\text{Turnover (sales)}}{\text{Finished goods and goods for resale}} = \frac{855.1}{159.3}\ (\text{£m}) = 5.368$$

So Electrocomponents converts into cash all of its finished goods and goods for resale around 5.4 times every year. To convert this figure into the number of days it takes to turn over these stocks, the original equation is inverted and multiplied by 365 days (or alternatively, 365 is divided by the stock turn figure: ie, 365/5.368 = 68 days):

$$\frac{\text{Finished goods and goods for resale}}{\text{Turnover (sales)}} = \frac{159.3}{855.1} \times 365 = 68$$

(£m: 159.3 / 855.1; Days: 68)

In summary, the company should be able to turn its end of year stock into cash in just over two months.

Taking the next class of current asset, debtors:

	£m
Debtors	168.9

Note 20 to the accounts states that debtors comprise:

Debtors	**£m**
Trade debtors	147.3
Amounts owing by subsidiary companies	-
Amounts owed by associated undertakings	0.5
Other debtors	4.7
Corporate tax	0.1
Prepaid catalogue expenses	9.9
Other prepayments and accrued income	4.1
Amounts falling due within one year	***166.6***
Other debtors falling due after more than one year	-
Corporate tax on profits	0.2
Prepaid pension costs	1.3
Other debtors	0.8
Total:	168.9

The very large majority of Electrocomponents' debtors are current trade debtors, falling due within one year, and below, how quickly these and the other debtors can be turned into cash will be examined.

As the company depends on sales to the trade, it is unlikely that they would be able to recall, or would want to recall, the £9.9 million in prepaid catalogue expenses, and the other amounts are not material. In summary then, £152 million of the £168.9 million in debtors would count towards the quick ratio.

In order to find out how quickly they would become cash, a similar calculation to that on the stock figure above is performed.

		£m		Times
$\dfrac{\text{Turnover (sales)}}{\text{Trade and other short term debtors}}$	=	$\dfrac{855.1}{152.0}$	=	5.626

So Electrocomponents converts its trade and other short-term debtors into cash around 5.6 times every year (which is 365/5.626 = 64.9 days), or:

		£m			Days
$\dfrac{\text{Trade and other short term debtors}}{\text{Turnover (sales)}}$	=	$\dfrac{152.0}{855.1}$	x 365	=	64.9

Therefore, the company should be able to turn its end of year debtors into cash again in just over two months.

Taking the next class of current asset, investments, Note 21 to the accounts states that all £6.7 million comprises bank deposits, which, unless they have been fixed for longer periods of time (this is unlikely, as the company has £75.5 million in debt) should be convertible into cash more or less immediately. Taken together with the £10.6 million cash at bank and in hand (which as stated elsewhere may be denominated in different currencies, but could, in extremis, be converted and repatriated if necessary) the company has £17.3 million in cash.

Summarising these current assets:

	£m	Days
Finished goods and goods for resale	159.3	68.0
Trade and other short term debtors	147.3	64.9
Bank deposits, cash at bank and in hand	17.3	0
	323.9	

Therefore, some 92% of Electrocomponents' current assets are convertible into cash in around 63 days, taking a weighted average number of days.

On further analysis, it is probable that some of the finished goods could be sold more quickly if discounts were offered to customers, but those discounts would reduce the amount of cash received. Also, the strict terms of trade of the company may require payment from trade debtors within 30 days, but some customers will not pay on time. It is possible that some of these debtors could be chased for more timely payment, or discounts could be offered for prompt payment. Therefore, if the company required more cash, it should be able to generate it from this balance sheet.

Looking at the other side of the quick ratio, the current creditors, a similar analysis can be performed.

	£m
Creditors: amounts falling due within one year	(202.1)

Note 22 to the accounts states that these creditors comprise:

Creditors: amounts falling due within one year	**£m**
Bank overdrafts (unsecured)	0.4
Current instalments of loans (See Note 24) ⋆	23.4
Trade creditors	71.8
Amounts owing to subsidiary companies	0
Corporate tax	24.4
Other taxation and social security	10
Other creditors	8.6
Government grants	0.1
Accruals and deferred income	22
Proposed dividend	41.4
Total:	202.1

⋆ Note 24 states that these are all foreign currency loans.

The creditor position is usually slightly more complicated than the debtor position.

It can be assumed that repayment of the unsecured overdrafts could be demanded immediately, although there is probably no reason why it should be. The current instalments of loans appears to refer to scheduled term loan repayments due during the next year, and although it could be assumed that only 2/12 of that figure might be repayable within the next two months, it is conventional to include all of it in the quick ratio, which generally will be taken to apply to assets and liabilities of under one year's term.

Trade creditors are always in the quick ratio, but it will be calculated below how quickly Electrocomponents pays its creditors and therefore how quickly cash will be required for this.

It can also be assumed that amounts owing to subsidiary companies will probably not be demanded immediately, but again they are included in the quick ratio calculation.

Corporate tax and other taxation and social security, accruals and deferred income and the proposed dividend are material figures and, though again probably not payable or repayable immediately, must be included in the quick calculation.

Other creditors will be included in the creditor days calculation below and the government grants figure will be included in the quick calculation, although it is not material.

To summarise the creditors:

Creditors: amounts falling due within one year	**£m**
Overdrafts & current instalments of loans	23.8
Trade & other creditors	80.4
Corporate & other taxation and social security	34.4
Government grants, accruals and deferred income	22.1
Proposed dividend	41.4
Total:	202.1

It was stated above that quick debtors were around £323.9 million (convertible to cash within around 63 days) and that quick creditors were around £202.1 million, leaving Electrocomponents Plc with £1.60 in highly liquid assets for every £1 owed in liabilities falling due within one year, which represents a quick liquidity ratio of 1.6: 1.

The immediacy of the cash requirement for most of these liabilities has been assessed, and it is reasonable to assume for example, that the loans will be payable evenly throughout the year. The tax and dividend payments requirement could be quite lumpy (ie, large and irregular) and may be payable at any time, but the government grants, accruals and deferred income are probably not repayable at all, and are accounting rather than cash adjustments. Creditors are a different matter and it is possible to analyse how long it takes for Electrocomponents Plc to pay its debts as follows (for this calculation, cost of sales is used rather than sales turnover):

$$\frac{\text{Cost of sales}}{\text{Trade \& other creditors}} = \frac{444.2}{80.4} = 5.525$$

(£m; Times)

So Electrocomponents pays all of its trade and other short-term creditors around 5.5 times every year, which is 365/5.525 = 66 days), or:

$$\frac{\text{Trade \& other creditors}}{\text{Cost of sales}} = \frac{80.4}{444.2} \times 365 = 66$$

(£m; Days)

In summary, Electrocomponents Plc gets paid by its customers before it pays its suppliers, which is a very healthy position to be in. It also has current and quick liquidity ratios of 1.74:1 and 1.6:1 respectively. These are harder ratios to assess in isolation and as always comparisons with other similar companies are more meaningful than absolute figures.

However, comparisons are difficult, because different companies in different sectors have very different balance sheets, none of them being typical either for businesses generally nor for other companies in the same business sector, though many will share some basic characteristics.

Manufacturers such as Electrocomponents Plc are also cited as examples of companies that carry a lot of stock and have quite large working capital requirements. If a manufacturer is selling into the retail sector, it is probably effectively holding stock for the retailers, who generally will order stock only days before they need it, often using just-in-time stock management software. When they order it, they will expect to be supplied immediately and, if this does not happen, they will lose sales, and may well change suppliers as a result.

This is why Electrocomponents Plc carries so much in the way of finished goods. It produces quite small value items for more than 1.5 million customers worldwide. It distributes them into the electrical, electronic, industrial, health and safety, and IT components markets principally through catalogues, CD-ROMS and websites. Their accounts state that:

"Because we serve users whose need is urgent, but whose orders are small, we have a large number of customers as well as a wide range of products, all of which must be available immediately."

However, manufacturers usually have suppliers who are on similar terms of trade as they are (say, one month) and as a result, will generally be able to match their debtors and creditors cash flows. As was seen with Electrocomponents, their debtors and creditors are liquidated every two months, within days of each other.

Retailers, especially food retailers, usually hold as little stock as they possibly can, and usually get paid for their sales immediately, whereas they often do not pay their suppliers for at least a month. This will leave them with low debtors, often high cash levels, and with low stock and debtor days in their balance sheets.

Alternatively, manufacturers of large capital items, such as Babcock International Group, (a large global process engineering and boiler making company) will have a completely different look to their balance sheet. Compare the key financial data from their 2001 report and accounts:

2001 Report & Accounts	**Electro-components**	**Babcock**
	£m	**£m**
Sales turnover	855.1	441.0
Cost of sales	(444.2)	(369.0)
PBIT (*after exceptional losses)	* 112.4	(11.0)
Fixed assets	353.3	114.7
Stocks	165.3	28.0
Debtors due within one year	166.6	98.8
Debtors due after one year	2.3	81.2
Investments, cash and bank balances	17.3	25.2
Creditors: due within one year	(202.1)	(199.3)
Current assets	***149.4***	***33.9***
Total assets less current liabilities	*502.7*	*148.6*
Creditors: due after one year	(76.6)	(2.5)
Provisions	(9.6)	(32.7)
Net assets	***416.5***	***113.4***

The liquidity calculations show the following:

	Electrocomponents	**Babcock**
Current liquidity:	1.74	1.17
Quick liquidity:	1.6	0.59
Debtor days:	64.9	73.3
Creditor days:	66.0	44.5

This is an interesting comparison as it shows that Babcock has to pay its suppliers much more quickly than it gets paid by its customers. This is to be expected because it purchases raw materials such as steel, cabling, etc, probably on one month's credit, and on average it will pay halfway through the month after receipt of the invoice, ie, around 45 days later. However, most of its sales are in heavy engineering (marine refitting, defence, generating, construction and rail care, etc) so delivery installation, commissioning and payment are quite slow compared with Electrocomponents.

The comparison also shows that Babcock is relatively illiquid compared to Electrocomponents, but Babcock is almost debt free and Electrocomponents has £75.5 million in debt, much of which is financing stocks, which Babcock doesn't need. This illustrates the differing liquidity requirements of different types of companies, demonstrating that it is important to look at each company on an individual basis and in the context of the liquidity requirements of its business.

Other types of companies, such as utilities, airlines, property companies, etc, have features such as high tangible fixed assets as a percentage of sales. Property companies will have high stock, debtor and creditor days (valuable stock, and few transactions that proceed slowly), whereas utilities companies tend to get paid fairly quickly and don't carry much stock.

These are just some of the general features of different types of sector balance sheets, but there is no such thing as a normal balance sheet, and differences between them could have relatively simple explanations.

For example, if one airline is more profitable than another, it may have lower gearing as a result of having generated more cash and therefore having less debt than its competitors. If one utility has made lots of acquisitions, it may have more goodwill in its balance sheet than other utilities do, because it has paid more for the acquired company's shares than the value of the underlying assets. The key thing is to isolate the important ratios and rationalise them against the business, to ensure that they are consistent with what the reports and accounts are saying about the business.

4.2 GEARING

Gearing refers to the relative proportions of debt and equity in the capital employed of a company. A company with more debt than equity is said to be highly-geared, and to have more equity than debt is low gearing.

Each form of finance has its benefits, but these benefits often have a downside. Equity is long-term, and generally doesn't get repaid. Debt can vary in term, but is usually more flexible than equity.

Equity can be cheap, as companies can decide the size of the dividend. Debt can be expensive, and interest has to be paid.

Shareholders will usually be happy with a low rate of return on their investment provided they share in capital growth, whereas lenders expect a higher rate of return on their debt as they don't share in capital growth.

Therefore, given a choice in the matter, companies will usually prefer to raise equity rather than debt, but this is not always possible. Although lenders usually have security, shareholders prefer to have a little more risk sharing in the financing of a business, and are therefore happy for the company to raise debt.

Different gearing profiles have an impact at different times of the business cycle. A highly geared company will be at risk during times of rising interest rates and economic slowdown, as higher interest costs associated with slower sales and cash generation are a big handicap. A company with more equity than debt will be at less financial risk, but might have unhappy shareholders who receive neither dividend nor capital growth.

In times of falling interest rates and rising economic activity, the reverse is true and a highly geared company starts to look attractive. Its interest costs fall, it can also repay debt early if necessary and shareholders receive a larger proportion of the capital gain from the shares, as it is mainly the debt that is generating growth, and lenders don't share in that growth.

Creditors are another possible source of finance which, theoretically at least, doesn't cost anything. The longer that is taken to pay them, the more cash can be conserved, and if sales debtors can be collected before the creditors are paid, its suppliers are effectively funding the company. We saw above how Electrocomponents takes 1.1 days more to pay its creditors than it takes to collect its debtors. This may be a small gap but on cost of sales of £444.2 million, it represents an interest benefit of £67,000 at an interest rate of 5%.

As always in accounting, the method by which gearing is calculated and what it means is matter of opinion, but what should be sought is an assessment of the financial and lending risk in the company. (Investors look for the business risk as well.) This can be achieved in a number of ways, the most frequently used of which are:

$$\text{Basic measure} = \frac{\text{Total debt}}{\text{Equity}} \times 100$$

$$\text{Widest measure} = \frac{\text{Total external liabilities}}{\text{Total assets}} \times 100$$

As demonstrated above, it sometimes takes a bit of detective work to figure out how much interest-bearing debt a company has on its books. Using Electrocomponents Plc as an example, a debt figure of £75.5 million was derived at 31 March 2001. In Chapter 1 Section 5.2 it was also seen that it has shareholders' funds of £416.5 million. A simple calculation therefore shows the debt gearing:

$$\frac{\text{Net debt}}{\text{Shareholders' funds}} = \frac{75.5}{416.5}\ (\text{£m}) = 18\%$$

It was stated above that Electrocomponents Plc is a relatively liquid company, which is borrowing primarily to finance the stocks that it needs to keep its customers supplied quickly. It has a relatively low gearing ratio, and as its debt is used to finance stocks, were the ratio to rise significantly, it might begin to cause concern that it was either over-stocked or not collecting its debts quickly enough.

Other companies that have a more heavily capital intensive business are likely to be more heavily geared, because they will tend to accumulate higher levels of debt by acquiring capital assets. Generally speaking, it is desirable when financing assets to match the type, term and amount of funding used to the assets being financed. Term debt or equity should fund fixed assets, and working capital finance should be used for working capital assets.

For example, if a heavy manufacturer requires a lot of heavy plant in its business, with a useful life of say, five to ten years, it is common to acquire these items of plant using finance leases of the same term (or operating leases if the assets are likely to have any residual value at the end of the lease). The financing of the asset will therefore amortise at the same rate that the assets wear out, and they also represent security in the event that the borrower defaults on the lease.

Similarly, property assets are acquired on very long leases (or mortgages) as they last longer than plant. IT equipment is generally purchased or acquired on very short leases, as it rapidly becomes obsolescent and has little residual value.

If items of goodwill are acquired (such as brands or other companies taken over at a premium to net asset value), it is generally more difficult to acquire on borrowed money and is typically classified as equity risk rather than debt risk. This is generally because there is little in the way of security that can be offered against such debt, and since lenders are very reluctant to take all of the risk on goodwill assets, shareholders will be required to provide more equity finance.

Working capital assets such as stocks or work in progress are generally financed using debt that is rapidly turned over, such as overdraft, bills of exchange, factoring or invoice discounting. It is also useful to have short-term debt so that any temporary surpluses of cash can be used to repay it immediately.

It would be very inefficient for a company to have a lot of term debt, probably on fixed interest rates or bearing heavy prepayment penalties, but to have cash on deposit at the same time, because the debt cannot be repaid. However, it should be noted that a company's gearing is not always representative of its business, nor will it necessarily be similar to other companies in the same sector. Whilst it is desirable to match the term of assets with the term of their funding, it is entirely possible that two companies in the same business sector could have very different debt to equity structures and therefore completely different gearing ratios.

For this reason, gearing also needs to be looked at in isolation, particularly when considering lending decisions. Highly geared companies are vulnerable to rising interest rates or slow cash generation, because they will have large interest bills to pay. Lenders will always want to ensure that their loans are serviced and repaid on time, without draining cash from the business that might be required to purchase raw materials necessary to generate business.

Typically they will seek to apply financial covenants to their loans, which will relate to cash generation for interest cover (see Section 4.3 below) and gearing. When applying gearing or net asset covenants, lenders try to apply limits that conform to industry norms, ie, if a business is capital intensive, gearing can be higher, say 50% to 100%. If it is in the retail sector, gearing should be lower, say between 25% and 33%. However, the senior covenant will always require strong generation of cash for the servicing of interest and the repayment of the debt.

4.3 INTEREST COVER

As stated above, interest cover is the term applied by lenders in their financial covenants to the relationship between free cash flow and net interest costs. It is a similar calculation to dividend cover, and lenders will usually require that cash flow (however measured) is at least 1.5 (and often more) times net interest costs. When applying this covenant, lenders may also seek to restrict dividend payments to ensure that the company does not pay shareholders before lenders.

4

FINANCIAL MANAGEMENT

Audited statutory accounts are usually published around three months after the end of each financial year. Companies are obliged to disclose material transactions or changes in circumstances which have occurred since the end of the year, but essentially the audited accounts are historical documents, and as stated above, have little practical value to company management.

The figures they use for day-to-day financial management are budgets, management accounts and forecasts.

Budgets are management's forecast of what the company will do over the next financial year. It is usually based on the previous year, but will usually assume some growth, along with changes such as new product development, new sites and changing headcount.

Budgets are phased for each of the twelve months of the financial year, and will contain P&L, cash flow and balance sheets at each period end. Phasing is vital because it shows maximum and minimum ranges for key figures such as cash or debt, which must be planned for.

Overheads and other fixed costs are relatively easy to budget for, as they are static, or at least, tend to change quite slowly. Sales are more difficult to budget for, as are variable costs of sales, and these items have a material effect on cash. Companies will assume that sales invoices will be paid according to their terms of trade (sometimes up to 60 days after invoicing) and will try to pay their suppliers as slowly as possible, often assuming 45 days credit (ie, on average, receipt of invoice in the middle of the month and payment at the end of the calendar month following the receipt of an invoice.) The impact of these cash flows is demonstrated in Chapter 2, Section 2 (debtors & creditors).

Management accounts are those through which the above transactions (sales, purchases, overheads and fixed costs) are processed. Each supplier, each cost, each department, each site and each product line will have its own account in the software package, and all transactions are painstakingly coded and entered into the relevant accounts.

They enable the accounting staff to keep track of each transaction posted into the accounts and also the overall performance of all the various elements in a company. It is possible for example, to monitor the profitability of individual sales lines and the costs of individual departments.

The management accounts still retain the same key elements as the report and accounts: a P&L statement, a balance sheet and a cash flow statement, and enable the tracking of financial performance against budget, forecast and prior year.

Anybody looking at the cumulative management accounts for the final month-end of the financial year will not be able to recognise them as relating to the same company as the statutory accounts, the annual report and accounts. It is also very difficult to reconcile any of the numbers in these two sets of accounts. This is not the result of the infamous keeping of two sets of books, but reflects the fact that many adjustments are made to the management accounts after the end of the year in order to produce the statutory accounts.

During the financial year, management accounts are produced showing monthly actuals, year-to-date and prior year figures.

Each variance is then analysed in order that the company can take action to correct the position or to ensure it is not caught out by events during the rest of the year. For example:

- sales might be under budget, so cash receipts would also be under, but fixed costs would probably be on budget, in which case working capital and overhead would be reviewed, and sales or prompt payment discounts offered to customers;
- capital expenditure may be under budget, which would imply that cash would be over budget, but would be

utilised more quickly during the rest of the year than originally forecast;

- debtor days might be over budget (ie, customers paying more slowly), and credit control might be strengthened or prompt payment discounts offered; or
- creditor days might be under budget (ie, the company paying its suppliers too quickly), and cash conservation exercises would be implemented.

Once the monthly and year-to-date variances have been understood, a new phased forecast would be prepared for the rest of the financial year, for comparison against actuals. The forecast becomes the living embodiment of the budget, as budgets are rarely formally revised. Monthly variances of forecast against actuals become more important as the year progresses and the budget becomes more out of date.

5

FINANCING METHODS AND CAPITAL MARKETS

Debt and equity financing have been referred to above, but it is worth briefly setting out the different types and sources of finance that companies can use, and which are disclosed in reports and accounts.

1. Equity

Equity is another name for the ordinary share capital of a company, subscribed by shareholders. It is the risk capital that a company receives in exchange for a share of the company and its profits, which also entitles the holder to any capital growth that it may achieve.

Generally speaking, anyone wishing to start or significantly expand a company must first raise some equity. In order to do this, they must prepare a business plan which states what the company is going to do, in which markets it intends to operate and which provides a three years sales and profit forecast and a summary of how much money is needed and what it is for.

Bearing in mind that equity investors can lose all of their investment if the company goes bust, the business or expansion plan must convince them that their equity will form part of a robust capital structure which will provide enough money for the business to run for several years, even in a worst case business scenario.

The equity in public companies is traded in the various stock markets around the world. In addition to the overseas markets such as NYSE and NASDAQ in the USA, the Paris, Frankfurt, Milan and Tokyo Stock Exchanges and the DAX in Germany, there are the LSE and the Alternative Investment Market (AIM) in London. This latter market is for shares in small companies, and because it does not have much liquidity, and because the level of disclosure for these companies is somewhat less onerous than on the main market, many bargains are done on a matched basis, ie, the shares are bought and sold by arrangement rather than through a broker that is holding shares on its own books.

There are also a number of indices for showing the state of each of the main global stock markets, although many people are probably more familiar with the names of the indices than they are with the names of the underlying markets. An index is a measure of the value of the shares making up the index, which will originally have started life at 100 and could subsequently rise or fall to any other number.

In the USA, the most famous index is the Dow Jones Industrial Average and the key index of the lesser NASDAQ market is the NASDAQ Composite. Germany has the Xetra Dax and Japan the NIKKEI. They are seen as such an important barometer of the economic health of nations that they are commonly heard on the national news, despite being fairly esoteric.

In the UK, there are a number of indices for the main board in addition to the Financial Times Stock Exchange index of the Top 100 shares by market capitalisation (FTSE 100) and the FT All Share Index (FTAS), which includes all shares quoted on the main board. These include the FTSE EuroTop 300 index of the top 300 European shares by market capitalisation.

As these indices are made up of the equity of companies ranked by market capitalisation, they can change. If a company's share price falls materially, it can be demoted from the FTSE 100, and vice versa. During the dot.com boom of the late 1990s, many so-called traditional stocks were demoted from the FTSE 100 to be replaced by dot.com companies whose shares had risen dramatically.

Of course, what followed was a dot.com bust, in which the FTSE declined as the underlying shares fell, until they fell so far that the constituent companies were demoted from the index to be replaced by the old traditional companies. Membership of the FTSE does grant a certain kudos, as it indicates that a company is amongst the 100 largest public companies in the UK. This can be a selling point for the shares, as the tracker funds, investment trusts that match the make-up of the relevant index, will have to buy its shares.

Equity can be structured in a myriad forms, each entitling the holder to different rights. Without going into every possible combination, here are the main types:

1.1 ORDINARY SHARES

These are the most common form of shares, and are very straightforward. Each share has a nominal value, but once it is authorised and issued, the value for which it can be sold will change according to various factors, such as the profitability of the company and the mood of the stock markets generally. The company's board authorises the shares, and when they want to raise some money, they issue the shares.

For example, a share with a nominal value of £1 would have formed part of the authorised share capital of the company when it was set up. If a million shares of £1 each have been authorised, then the so-called authorised share capital of the company is £1 million. If only half of those shares are issued, then the authorised and issued share capital will be £500,000.

However, that is probably the only time that the share will be valued at £1. As soon as the company decides to issue and sell the shares, their value will change. For example, on an initial public offering (IPO) the company may decide that the £1 shares are worth £2, perhaps because the market in their sector is buoyant and the IPO represents a good investment opportunity. If they manage to sell all the shares for £2, then the equity part of the balance sheet will appear as follows:

Capital and Reserves	£000
Called up share capital	1,000
Share premium account	1,000
Profit & loss account	0
Other reserves	0
Equity share owner's funds	**2,000**

From the day that the shares are sold the price can change, so someone who paid £2 for a share on Day 1 can sell it for £3 the next day. The additional cash goes to the shareholder who sold the share, not to the company, which is why, as explained above, a company's market capitalisation (the value of all its ordinary shares) can differ so much from its balance sheet shareholders' funds.

In the UK, all ordinary shares must have a par value and cannot be issued at a discount to (ie, less than) that value, which is why many ordinary shares in issue have low par (nominal or face) values. They can subsequently trade at a discount to their par value. In the USA, shares do not need to have par values and can be sold for any amount.

1.2 PREFERENCE SHARES

As the name implies, these are shares that have some form of preferential status over the ordinary shares, usually connected with dividend rights.

Holders of preference shares must be paid their dividends, usually a fixed amount that cannot be changed by the directors, before those of the ordinary shares. Preference shares can also be subdivided into other classes.

- Cumulative preference shares
  If for any reason the company does not pay the preference dividend, the dividend accumulates until such time as they can pay it. The dividend is then said to be in arrears and the accounts must note that this liability exist, as it may affect the company's ability to pay ordinary dividends.
- Convertible preference shares
  These are preferred shares which carry the right to convert to ordinary shares at some specified future date (or dates, or for a time period between two dates) and at a specified rate (say 10 ordinary shares for each preference share).
- Redeemable preference shares
  These are preferred shares which the company must redeem (repay in cash) at a future point in time. This makes them similar to debt, but they carry the right to receive a preferred dividend rather than bear interest. They are often used in situations, often in highly geared or restructuring situations, where the company cannot

afford to pay interest, but may at some point be able to pay dividends. In this situation, they will usually be cumulative redeemable preference shares.

- Participating preference shares
  These are preferred shares in which the holder receives a variable share of the ordinary dividend as well as the preferred dividend.

1.3 SHARE VALUATIONS

As stated above, there is little direct comparison between the market value of a company (ie, its market capitalisation) and net worth shown in the accounts. However, anyone who owns shares in a quoted company does not refer to the accounts to find out how much they are worth, they check the price of the shares on stock exchange on which they are listed.

The shareholders also know that they can generally sell the shares at any time, except if dealings in the shares are suspended for any reason. Big stock exchanges are usually very liquid, and there is no problem with buying or selling shares, and this liquidity in the shares is a compelling reason for having them listed on a large market.

Potential investors would look at the accounts when considering buying the shares, to look at things such as profitability, growth, gearing, and other key financial performance measures, but a key figure would be the dividend. The interim and final dividends per share are disclosed in the accounts, and a simple calculation of this dividend divided by the share price over 100 would show the dividend yield, a key investment criterion. The dividend figure disclosed in the accounts is intended to be maintained for the short term, as reducing it would have a material negative impact on the share price, leaving the company vulnerable to a takeover.

Smaller markets such as AIM or over-the-counter (OTC) markets are less liquid, and transactions in their listed shares are often only possible on a matched bargain basis, where the shares can only be sold directly by the owner to a new owner, and would not be taken onto the books of an intermediary or jobber in the meantime. However, it is still possible to trade these shares where there are willing buyers, and the dividend would still be a key factor in the valuation.

Potential investors might decide that, in exchange for the risk in holding shares that they could not readily sell, they would like a dividend yield of, say 25%. In this instance, they would divide the dividend per share by 25, and multiply the result by 100 to indicate the price they would be willing to pay per share. Potential investors will always expect a higher return from an illiquid share because, in addition to the shares not being very easy to value or sell, earnings are likely to be more volatile, leaving the dividend payment vulnerable.

There is an even bigger problem with selling shares in private companies, which is that with the shares in private hands, and the company probably being managed by the owners of the shares, there is no guarantee that there will be any dividend at all. In this case, a share valuation would be based partly on the accounts, particularly past financial performance and track record, and partly on the nature of the business.

Analysis of the accounts and past financial performance will demonstrate whether the company has been profitable, has generated cash and has a strong balance sheet. A review of the company's management, its products and its competitive position will give an indication of whether it will continue to perform strongly. A review of the business will potentially indicate a basis for valuation.

For example, asset valuations could be used for companies with an assets-based business, such as an investment property company, provided the valuations are reasonably up-to-date.

Companies with few assets are more difficult to value, and some formula related to sustainable cashflow or profits would be required. For example, if a private company has made average pre-tax profits of £1 million for the previous five years, it might be reasonable to assume that it will continue to do so for the foreseeable future. Even if the profits are not distributed as dividends, they will either be retained as cash or ploughed back into the business, in which case, they arguably add to the value of the investment.

Anyone buying shares in a private company would press for dividends to be paid, or alternatively discount the price being offered for the shares to reflect that fact that dividends are not paid. Anyone buying sufficient shares in a private company to be able to control whether it pays dividends or not would have to pay a premium for such control.

Ridiculous prices were paid for the shares of start-up internet, technology and web-based companies on the assumption that their growth rates would mirror the fantastic growth rate of the internet itself. However, these companies were still in the same business as companies using traditional sales channels, and the internet companies usually proved no better than the competition or were trying to sell into depressed markets. There have been some outstanding successes and some amazing failures, but in the main, the ridiculous share prices paid for shares did not mirror the value of the business, and all that really happened was that the founders made astounding sums of money and later shareholders paid the price.

2. Debt

Debt is the other main source of finance for companies, once they have raised as much equity as they can. As described elsewhere, the proportion of debt to equity is known as gearing, and it has a substantial impact on the financial performance of a company and on its ability to raise further finance.

There are many different types of debt, the main ones being:

Loan finance

Loan finance comes in many forms, ranging from long-term debt to short-term overdraft finance. As described elsewhere, the term of the finance should equate as closely as possible to the life of the assets being financed. Long-term debt can be fixed for as much as 25 years (eg, mortgage debentures, used for property) or as little as one year.

Overdraft, or other forms of short-term debt finance, is repayable on demand and an overdraft facility will usually be granted for 364 days or less. Short-term debt is also available through bills of exchange, acceptance credits or commercial paper facilities. All of these are simply forms of paper that lenders take in exchange for the debt.

Commercial paper

Commercial paper is like a post-dated cheque, in that it is an instrument drawn by the borrower for a fixed amount. Unlike a cheque however, it has a maturity date and is negotiable, and the issuer authorises the sale of the paper via the bank holding the facility. Commercial paper is mainly taken up by corporates as a form of short-term investment, as the commercial paper issues will have received a credit rating from one of the ratings agencies.

Bills of exchange/acceptance credits

These are similar to commercial paper, in that they consist of a written instrument that is a promise by the borrower to repay the lender a fixed sum of money on a fixed forward date. They come in two main forms: ineligible bills and acceptance credits.

Ineligible or trade bills of exchange are given to suppliers by purchasers in exchange for goods, usually for presentation and payment in 30 days' time. This is simply a form of deferred consideration, (ie, trade credit), and has the same effect as the supplier handing over the goods along with an invoice saying "Payment due in 30 days time" (ie, open account). In both cases, the supplier has an asset, but no money as yet.

However, in both cases, the supplier can turn the asset into cash by borrowing against it. It can either factor or discount the invoice (see below) or it can discount the trade bill (ie, borrow against it). The trick with the latter option is to find someone willing to pay cash for the bill and take the risk that the issuer of the bill will be able to pay when it falls due. These are ineligible bills, and have been used for centuries to finance trade.

Eligible bills of exchange (acceptance credits) are quite different. They are the same type of instrument (ie, a promise by the borrower to pay the lender a fixed sum of money on a fixed forward date) but they are drawn for general trade purposes, and not against a specific trade transaction.

Companies complete the written instrument with their name, the amount (usually fixed sums in £millions), the term (usually 30 to 90 days) and the objects clause (ie, the purpose for which they are borrowing the money to finance, which is usually inventory or receivables). The inchoate bills are then signed by authorised company signatories and kept at the bank. When the company wishes to borrow some money, it authorises the bank to issue the bills (ie, put a drawn date on them) and to pay the discounted proceeds into their bank account.

Facility types

Bank facilities can be arranged in very many forms, encompassing each of the above forms of debt individually or combining them in revolving credit facilities, which could include other facilities such as:

- money market borrowings (short term loans for fixed periods from one week up to one year);
- bonds and guarantees (and other transactions variously described as undertakings); and
- foreign currency dealing facilities.

Long-term debt can also be designated as senior debt (which ranks above all other forms of loan finance) or subordinated debt (which ranks behind all other loans).

Term debt facilities can be syndicated (ie, the leading bank can either form a syndicate of lenders at the start or can set up the facility then sell down parts of the facility to other banks) and the other banks can then be formed into a tender panel, in which each of the lenders can bid for new tranches of debt.

Thus a borrower can have a secure facility with a number of different lenders, thereby spreading its exposure, and it can usually rely on getting the lowest rates in the market, because it can solicit bids from the lenders in its tender panel which may have a greater appetite for lending or for exposure to that borrower.

Long-term debt can also be issued as convertible into equity at pre-determined rates, and either dates or periods of time. It can also be issued as loan stock or some form of fixed or floating rate notes, which might be secured or unsecured, or convertible, and which can then be traded in debt markets.

Mezzanine finance

This is a generic term for a type of convertible debt that is used to finance high risk companies, such as start-ups or venture capital investments. If such high risk companies cannot raise sufficient equity to be able to attract lenders (lenders don't want to take all of the risk in a company and want to see that shareholders have taken a bigger risk first) or if existing or potential equity investors consider the equity risk to be too high, they will subscribe to this form of debt.

It is usually long-term, subordinated debt, but it is convertible to equity at some point during its term (usually at the lender's behest, depending on the share price). In the meantime, it bears a higher rate of interest than other more senior debt, in order to reflect the additional risk borne by the lender whilst the debt is subordinated and in view of the fact that the share price may never rise high enough to warrant or trigger conversion to equity.

Leasing, HP, securitisation

Other forms of term debt are usually leases or hire purchase related to fixed assets such as property, plant, machinery, etc, or securitisation of financial assets such as income streams (eg, music publishing, performance or recording royalties, such as the famous Bowie bond) or debt books (eg, mortgages, hire purchase agreements and credit card debts).

All of the forms of loan and mezzanine finance should appear as liabilities on a company's balance sheet, but at present, there is scope to take some forms of lease finance off balance sheet, in other words, not to show either the finance or the financed assets on the balance sheet. These issues are currently being reviewed by the Accounting Standards Board and it is widely expected that a new standard will be released which will eliminate such distinctions and compel all companies to put all forms of debt on their balance sheet.

Factoring and invoice discounting

Factoring and invoice discounting are financing techniques usually associated with very cash-strapped companies, but they are very common forms of assets-backed debt, the assets in this case being trade receivables. When a company issues an invoice to accompany a sale, it can wait anything up to three months to get paid. Some companies cannot wait that long, but do not have access to sufficient overdraft facilities to finance their debtors for that period of time, so they sell the invoice along with the right to receive the cash.

In both cases, the buyer of the debts pays a discounted amount up front, but with invoice discounting, the buyer of the debtors gets paid the cash when the seller receives it, and with factoring, the buyer takes responsibility for collecting the debt and accounting for the debtors. In either case, it is expensive and often a last resort. However, it can be useful for young companies that have yet to establish their business or raise more senior finance.

6

FINANCIAL RISK MANAGEMENT

Some key financial risks, the management of which will often be referred to in the accounts follow.

1. Interest Rate Exposure

Interest rate exposure is the potential effect on the P&L arising from interest rate changes that may affect the income and cash flow from financial assets, or which may cause an increase in the cost of debt servicing. This exposure is usually managed by fixing or floating interest rates.

If a company is borrowing in a rising interest rate environment or, investing in a falling environment, it will try to fix its interest rates so borrowing costs are capped and investment income protected. If it is investing in a rising interest rate environment or borrowing in a falling environment, it will try to float its interest rates to take advantage of higher investment income or falling interest costs as soon as possible. More sophisticated exposure managers use interest rate swaps, Forward Rate Agreements (FRAs), interest rates futures, or various new forms of financial derivatives.

2. Foreign Exchange Risk

Foreign Exchange risk is essentially an exposure to a currency other than the base reporting and operating currency of the company, either from sale or purchase transactions in other currencies (transaction exposure), having assets and liabilities in other currencies (translation or balance sheet exposure) or having strategic or economic exposure to other currencies (eg, having a major competitor operating from a country with different base currency).

3. Refinancing Risk

Refinancing risk is the risk that a company may not be able to renew or replace its debt facilities when they expire. Debt facilities will always carry an expiry date, from the usual 364 days of an unsecured overdraft facility to 5 years or more for a large revolving credit facility. A prudent treasurer will start negotiating the renewal or replacement of such facilities well in advance of their expiry, to ensure that they will be available continuously to the company.

To demonstrate the effect of refinancing risk, when news of the Enron fraud broke, many of its loan facilities went into default as they breached financial covenants their loan agreements. At the same time, ratings agencies (such as Moody's and S&P) downgraded Enron's debt securities and this downgrade triggered default clauses in those securities. With all of its debt facilities being withdrawn just as it needed them, its collapse was very swift.

4. Credit Risk

Credit risk is the risk of customers defaulting on their debts or of sustaining losses from defaults on investments. Credit risk is managed by undertaking due diligence on customers before trading with them, by effective credit control and debtor chasing or by using guaranteed forms of payment by customers until such time as their credit is assured.

5. Investment Risk

Investment risk is managed by limiting investment to approved investment counterparties and approved investment instruments. Companies typically establish an investment policy, which covers approved financial instruments (degree of capital risk), credit ratings (degree of counterparty risk), investment term (time and liquidity risk) and amount (counterparty position risk).

7

INTERNATIONAL ACCOUNTING

1. Introduction

One of the consequences of the globalisation of financial markets is that increasingly, companies are seeking listings on overseas stock markets, especially in countries where they have either material investments or markets. In addition to increasing the liquidity of their shares, it gives them access to wider and larger capital markets. For UK companies this has usually meant seeking additional listings in the USA, one of the UK's biggest markets, and also the source of huge amounts of private and institutional capital.

However, this has significantly increased the amount of disclosure and/or involved a material reworking of financial reports and accounts, because of the different and stricter reporting standards and requirements in the USA.

European accounting standards have always been much closer to UK standards, partly because of the existence of a common legal system (the Roman system) and partly because the UK boasts a more sophisticated financial infrastructure, which has been followed rather than led. The development of the European Union has accelerated convergence between European countries, so there are few material differences in accounting and reporting standards.

A key factor however is the existence of EU directives on accounting and company law which require that member states pass them into their own legislation, indicating that as well as being a force for convergence in accounting standards, the EU will require those standards to be enshrined in law.

The IASC was established in 1973 to formulate and promote uniformity in the content and presentation of financial statements. Many accountancy bodies worldwide are member of the IASC, and they have all agreed to support IASC standards and to promote compliance.

IASC standards generally recognise US practices, modified by accepted practice in other countries. This is a difficult area because there is rarely a consensus among standard setters as to the best practice to adopt, and there is little commonality between US standards and the rest of the world. Where IASC standards have achieved common usage, this seems to indicate that the various international standards are actually much closer to each other than might seem to be the case.

Notwithstanding this, international standards have no direct application in the UK, and only UK GAAP needs to be consulted by UK companies at present. However, international accounting standards must be implemented for EU listed companies with effect from 2005, and for prior year comparatives in 2004, which is likely to cause great difficulty for analysts in attempting to maintain meaningful historical comparatives.

2. Current Main Differences between UK and US GAAP

Broadly speaking, US accounting standards (set by the FASB) are much more prescriptive than UK or European standards, although they do still call for judgement to be exercised in their application. Furthermore, these accounting standards are enshrined in law, whereas most UK and European standards are not. Thus the US is said to have a rules-based approach, which is largely prescriptive.

In the UK, Companies Acts legislation simply requires UK accounts to represent a true and fair view of the state of a company's affairs, and the accounting standards prescribe how to achieve this. This is described as a principles-based approach, in which guidance is offered by the ASB as to how to approach accounting issues, but leaves the actual treatment to the discretion of the directors, provided the outcome is true and fair.

Although the above distinction generally holds good, the massive accounting scandals and frauds perpetrated in the USA in early 2002 demonstrate that, even with a tough legal and accounting framework, people involved in the management of public companies can still make big profits forecasts and then have to cheat in order to achieve them. In other cases, they manipulate profit to trigger bonus or other incentive payments for their own benefit.

In addition to being part of the culture of greed, these activities are symptomatic of the short-termism that affects all stock markets, in which share price rises are the key indicator that the investor is interested in, rather than long-term growth or even dividend yield. An inevitable conclusion is that there is nothing wrong with the system; it is the people employed in it who are at fault.

FASB's standards are enforced by the SEC, a government agency, and in addition to compliant reports and accounts, US companies also have to disclose much more information than is required in the UK. This disclosure must either appear in the reports and accounts or be filed with the SEC in a separate document called the 10K.

Many companies that have significant activity or shareholdings in the US produce a summary of the impact of US GAAP on their accounts, which in some cases is highly material, both in terms of net assets and earnings, and therefore on performance measures such as earnings per share.

If UK companies want to attract US investors without going through the complications of an additional listing, they produce a reconciliation of their accounts to US GAAP, showing how the material elements of the accounts will be affected by the different treatments. They may also show a translation of the UK accounts into US dollars (or Euros, for European markets).

There follow some examples of the main differences between UK and US GAAP.

1.1 GOODWILL AND INTANGIBLE FIXED ASSETS

As described above, goodwill and other intangible fixed assets are a vexatious issue in the accounting world.

The concepts of a brand name as an intangible fixed asset and goodwill as the difference between the fair value attributed to an investment in business or a subsidiary undertaking and the fair value of the underlying net assets at the date of their acquisition have already been described above.

Under UK GAAP, since 1 January 1998, judgement can be exercised as to how quickly these assets can be written off, or as was seen with the WPP accounts for the period to 31 December 2000, retained indefinitely on the balance sheet. Prior to 1 January 1998, goodwill was immediately written off.

Under US GAAP, goodwill in respect of 'business combinations accounted for as purchases' (ie, acquisitions) should be written off over its useful life, which should not be more than 40 years. Goodwill acquired by other means or accounted for differently would not be recognised under US GAAP.

As a consequence of adjusting for these differences, the shareholders' funds for WPP as at 31 December 2000 under UK GAAP were £3,409.9 million, whereas under US GAAP, they were £4,191.1 million, a difference of almost 23%.

1.2 SHARE CONSIDERATION

If a company's shares are used to acquire other companies, under UK GAAP, the price of the shares on the date that the acquisition becomes effective is the price used to measure the consideration paid for the acquisition. Under US GAAP, it is the share price at the date of the announcement that is used to measure the consideration.

1.3 CONTINGENT CONSIDERATION

Contingent consideration is further payment to the vendors (usually of private company shares) for an acquisition, and is contingent upon the achievement of financial performance targets, usually called an earn-out. In this way, the acquirer can ensure that vendors tied to the acquired company will keep working effectively for it, as they will receive more money for doing so.

Under UK GAAP, contingent consideration is only accounted for as a liability when the likelihood of its payment becomes 'probable' (a fine judgement, but presumably based on financial performance prior to and near the end of the earn out period). It can also be accounted for as additional purchase consideration for the acquisition.

Under US GAAP, contingent consideration is only accounted for as a liability when the likelihood of its payment passes 'beyond reasonable doubt.'

(The distinction between probable and beyond reasonable doubt is a small one. The Oxford English Dictionary defines probable as meaning likely, possible, plausible, feasible, believable, credible, conceivable, tenable, expected. Likely is at one end of this scale, and expected at the other, but none of them imply beyond reasonable doubt, which indicates the extent of the range of judgements that may be used in these matters.)

Also, under US GAAP, contingent consideration has to be accounted for as compensation (ie, remuneration) for the vendors.

1.4 DIVIDENDS

Under UK GAAP, the dividend recommended by the directors is shown on the face of the P&L, but only becomes a liability of the company once the shareholders have approved it.

Under US GAAP, the recommended dividend is only provided for in the accounts once the legal obligation to pay it has arisen, ie, when the dividend is declared.

1.5 DEFERRED TAX

In the UK, deferred tax is accounted for under FRS 19. Broadly speaking, deferred tax is only recognised in the accounts when the underlying timing differences are expected to reverse.

Under US GAAP, deferred tax is established on all timing differences, and a valuation allowance is established in relation to deferred tax assets if it is more likely than not that some portion will remain unrealised. In other words, even though it may never be realised, some proportion of the deferred tax asset can be recognised in the accounts, in contrast to other items, which are only recognised in the accounts when they are either realised or realisable.

1.6 EXECUTIVE COMPENSATION

This difference relates to the acquisition of a company's own shares for the purposes of employee compensation. Under US GAAP, such compensation is measured at the fair value of the shares at the time that the performance criteria are met or the award of shares as compensation is vested (becomes payable) with the employee.

If UK companies acquire shares for employee compensation schemes, it is possible that they can be acquired prior to the award being vested, and therefore the value of the compensation will be established at that point rather than when the award is actually made.

Furthermore, under UK GAAP, any increase in the value of the shares between the date of acquisition and the date of vesting will not give rise to a charge to the P&L, whereas it could under US GAAP.

1.7 CASH FLOW

Under the UK standard FRS 1, the cash flow statement must set out the source of cash under the following classifications:

a) operating activities (profit before interest and tax);
b) returns on investment and servicing of financing (interest);
c) taxation;
d) investing activities (capital expenditure);
e) equity dividends paid; and
f) financing activities (borrowing or lending money.

Under the equivalent US accounting standard SFAS 95, cash flow only needs to be set out as follows:

a) operating activities (profit before interest and tax);
b) investing activities (capital expenditure); and
c) financing activities (borrowing or lending money.

Returns on investment and servicing of financing, taxation and equity dividends paid are all considered financing activity under the US standard. Additionally, payments made against provisions set up in respect of acquisitions (eg, provisions for restructuring costs, etc) are accounted for in the UK as investment activities (as they relate to investments in subsidiaries) but under the US standard, they are regarded as operating cash flows.

1.8 EMPLOYEE SHARE OWNERSHIP PLANS (ESOPS)

These are share ownership programmes set up by employers in order that employees may invest in the shares of their employers or receive compensation in shares. Generally speaking, companies set up ESOP trusts that acquire these shares and hold them until such time as the obligation arises to vest them in employees.

Under UK GAAP, shares purchased by the ESOP are recorded as fixed asset investments at cost, less amounts written off. Under US GAAP, shares purchased by the ESOP are recorded at cost and deducted from the share owner's equity.

1.9 LISTED INVESTMENTS

Under UK GAAP, if companies own listed shares which comprise less than 20% of the share capital of the issuer, the investment is held in the accounts at cost, minus any provision made for any diminution in value.

Under US GAAP, such investments can be classified as either:

a) trading;
b) available for sale; or
c) held to maturity.

Trading investments must be stated at fair value, with gains and losses going to earnings. Available for sale investments would be marked to market (ie, re-valued) and any gain or loss on the value taken to shareholders' funds. Held-to-maturity investments must be stated at amortised cost.

Any permanent diminution in value of any of these investments would be taken through the P&L under both accounting conventions.

1.10 ACCOUNTING FOR DERIVATIVES AND HEDGING ACTIVITIES

Hedging activities and the use of derivatives were referred to in Chapter 6, and are basically methods of managing foreign currency and interest rate risk. Accounting for them has always been difficult, as they are complicated transactions.

A new, highly complicated, prescriptive and controversial US accounting standard, FASB 133 requires all hedge transactions (including any instruments embedded in other transactions, eg, the implicit sale of a currency put option in a dual currency deposit) to be recorded in the balance sheet as an asset or liability, measured at its fair value.

Changes in the hedge's value must be taken into the P&L unless specific criteria are met. These criteria are that the hedge must relate precisely to an underlying financial exposure in the accounts, and this matched position must be designated and clearly documented, and the effectiveness (ie, its ability to match the underlying position) monitored and assessed. If this process is carried out, then any gains or losses on the underlying exposure (which should roughly equal and offset gains and losses on the hedging transaction) can be taken to the P&L.

Previously, treasurers were able to use hedging strategies on economic exposures, in which no current or tangible financial exposures existed. In future, these types of hedging transactions will be treated the same way as trading derivatives for profit, and will be accounted for through the P & L.

Very few UK companies have yet to implement FASB 133, but if they do, it will be expected to make their earnings more volatile, as such changes in the value of hedges were not previously accounted for until the underlying position was unwound or the exposure was recognised in the accounts.

The matching international and UK standards, IAS39 and FRED23, will also be coming into effect during the next two years. There is a debate as to why the UK should adopt FRED 23 in 2003 before switching to IAS39 in 2005, and there are still issues of principle between IAS39 and FAS 133 to be resolved, so watch this space.

1.11 PENSION COSTS

In the UK, companies used to account for pension costs under SSAP 24, which allowed them to charge the costs over the employees' working lives. However, FRS 17 has much stricter requirements that have caused many problems for UK companies, especially those with final salary pension schemes. The new standard has caused many companies to drop final salary schemes for new entrants because of the enormous impact that the fluctuation of the value of such funds and liabilities has on their annual results.

Under US GAAP, pension costs are determined under SFAS 87 and 88, which essentially charge these costs to earnings. Moreover, differing actuarial methods and assumptions are used, along with different methods of amortising pension fund surpluses or deficits. These differences have had a material effect on some bigger companies, as pension costs can represent an enormous cost. Some US company results announced in 2001 and 2002 included losses in the tens of billions of dollars as a result of these changes.

1.12 ACCOUNTING FOR REDUNDANCIES

Under UK GAAP, in calculating incremental pension benefits in respect of workforce reductions, costs are taken into account when determining future pension costs, unless the fund is currently in deficit (ie, it will not be able to meet all its estimated pension liabilities in the future). In this case, the additional pension costs needed to meet the liabilities arising from workforce reductions are taken to the P&L in the year in which the reductions occur.

Under US GAAP, the cost of providing incremental pensions benefits for redundant workers is taken to earnings in the financial year in which the redundancies are agreed.

1.13 CAPITALISATION OF INTEREST

As described elsewhere, this is one of the key areas of judgement in UK accounting, and can have a highly material impact on earnings. Under UK GAAP, wide scope exists for companies to decide how much interest is directly attributable to the asset on which expenditure has occurred, and there is no prescribed term over which the asset itself must be written off.

Under US GAAP, any capitalised interest must be added to fixed assets and written off over the life of the asset, which must not exceed 40 years.

8

CURRENT & FUTURE ISSUES

Even a brief look at the ASB's website shows an enormous amount of work in progress and it would be futile to list all of the current issues under review as they will be out of date almost immediately.

However, the main issues currently being addressed are the attempts to codify international accounting standards and to harmonise them globally. There are many unresolved or unsatisfactory issues still to be dealt with in the UK alone, and because of the many different viewpoints and entrenched positions, resolving them will be a long process.

Following on from the recent corporate debacles in the USA, eg, the massaging of profits by the gigantic corporation, AOL Time Warner, it seems unlikely that harmonisation will happen in the near future. A far more pressing requirement in all jurisdictions is to enshrine accounting standards in company law, so that knowingly breaching them for personal or corporate gain is punishable as a crime.

The largest and most complex individual issues are:

- accounting for derivatives (the new US standard FASB 133 is widely regarded as fundamentally flawed and far too difficult to understand);
- removing the distinction between operating and finance leases, so that all leases and matching assets are on the balance sheet;
- accounting for pension costs in a manner that does not have a huge impact on the P&L as the value of the invested funds rises and falls with the markets.

Once those issues have been resolved, doubtless others will replace them.

9

CONCLUSION

There are three main pillars holding up the rules and processes behind the production of company reports and accounts: accounting standards (and implicitly, company law), audit and corporate governance.

1. Accounting Standards

Today's global businesses and the transactions they undertake are complex and daily becoming more complex. Accounting for them is not simple and neither is the process of deciding what the principles behind the accounting treatment should be. This is why, some 500 years after Paccioli started trying, there is still no harmonised global accounting infrastructure.

Accounting standards are the outcome of the tensions and the relationships between standard setters, the profession and the practitioners, and there is apparently little room for compromise. In order to accommodate everybody's ideas, and to cope with accounting principles and rules being needed for every conceivable situation, massive scale and complexity are the inevitable result.

Even though accounting standards are complex and lengthy, and have been honed following wide and long consultation, company accounts are still opaque, despite years of determined work by the ASB. They are not user-friendly, even to practitioners, and despite the plethora of guidance, rules and legislation, companies are still able to show matters in the most favourable light and will bend the rules as far as possible in order to achieve this.

Understandably, governments and regulators have now stepped into the arena in force. An article in the Sunday Times of 8 December 2002 quoted a practitioner as wryly noting that 34 separate enquiries into financial reporting were currently running, but there was no Office of Fair Trading (OFT) competition inquiry into the big four accounting firms.

Much hope and expectation surrounds the current move towards convergence of international accounting standards. The 7,000 quoted companies in Europe are due to start using these standards by 2005 and the International Accounting Standards Board (IASB) has also reached a ground-breaking agreement with the US Federal Accounting Standards Board, opening the way for the convergence of European and US accounting standards at some point in the future.

However, convergence is a two-edged sword.

It will be an incredibly difficult process to achieve because US and IASB standards are based on rules and UK standards are based on principles. If UK companies do adopt IASB or US standards, it will entail a tremendous upheaval, especially because of some of the provisions of the Sarbanes-Oxley Act, recently introduced in the US.

This act was designed to restore investor confidence in financial reporting and requires enhanced disclosure, and greater auditor independence and objectivity, aided by an increased role for independent audit committees in dealing with auditors. There are concerns in the UK that some of the provisions of this Act contravene UK company law, so UK companies that are listed in the USA may be breaking UK law by complying with US law in their reporting.

The three main areas of difference between UK, US and IASB standards are accounting for pensions, derivatives and stock options. If IASB standards are accepted, it will introduce tremendous volatility to UK and European company accounts, and will probably reduce profits overall. Paradoxically, the outcome of the proposed derivatives accounting rules will probably re-introduce the volatility in company profits that currency and interest rate hedging were initially designed to eliminate.

Furthermore, increased volatility, reduced profit levels and changing accounting policies will make it impossible to carry out any meaningful comparisons with company, sector or stock exchange index performance in the past. Standard setters and regulators alike are concerned that this may lead to the widespread disposal of equity investments until investors understand and become comfortable with the rules and their impact on financial reporting.

There is one immediate controversy that will highlight the problems of convergence. The IASB has issued proposals that will end the UK practice of merger accounting, a popular ruse that allows a company taking over another to include profits from the acquirer and target company for the year in which the merger occurs. Under acquisition accounting, only the profits from the target company from the point at which it was acquired can be included in the accounts. Furthermore, merger accounting does not give rise to the large amounts of goodwill that arise in acquisitions when the acquirer pays more to acquire the shares of a company than the net book value of its assets. Merger accounting has already been banned in the USA because of the kinds of widespread abuse previously seen in the UK.

In addition, many UK loan agreements contain frozen GAAP covenants. This means that whenever they change accounting policies, if the change has an impact on the monitoring and measurement of financial performance against cashflow or profit covenants, the accounts have to be restated using the original policies. This creates a huge amount of extra work and complexity, and increased risk for lenders and borrowers alike.

Reports and accounts may not be perfect, but they are probably as good as can be achieved at the moment. Standard setters take the view that there is not much wrong with the rules: it's the way that they are applied that is the problem. However, they also recognise that there is a long way to go in terms of ensuring maximum disclosure, transparency and uniformity (though not necessarily clarity) but great hopes are placed in the planned convergence of IASB, US and UK standards, which if nothing else, should bring about greater uniformity and comparability in financial reporting.

2. Audit

The Bannerman case in July 2002 has led audit firms to seek to include disclaimers in their reports to the effect that they neither accept nor assume any responsibility for any other purpose to which the accounts may be put, nor to any other person to whom the reports and accounts are shown. Given the disrepute that recent cases have brought to the accounting profession, this latest attempt to disclaim responsibility for any reliance being placed on company accounts is worrying.

It comes after several accounting scandals that have cost many employees, pensioners, creditors and investors enormous amounts of money. It has also been noticed that the company directors and managers at the helm at the time of the collapse of their companies have not only not been prosecuted and imprisoned, but have managed to hang onto most of their ill-gotten gains. Under these circumstances, people have a right to ask "Who is actually responsible for this?"

Auditors have long been thought to lack objectivity in their audits. Auditors report to the very same directors that appoint them and then agree their fees. Audit partners' drawings and profit share depend on happy clients, and qualified accounts do not make for happy clients. Partnership profits have been inflated by lucrative consultancy work for audit clients, so the effect of the loss of an audit could be huge. Furthermore, how many auditor partners would disagree with their own consulting partners about whether the tax schemes or balance sheet structures that the client paid for do not really work?

These conflict of interest issues have been exacerbated by the many mergers between accounting firms that have taken place over the last ten years, followed by the collapse of Arthur Andersen. There are now only four UK firms ostensibly large enough to be able to undertake the massive logistical task of auditing a global multinational. Although some of these firms are now disposing of or de-merging their consulting arms, they are increasingly able to act as a cartel in terms of setting fee rates. Since an auditor's learning curve is very steep with a new client, dramatically increasing their risk for the first two to three years, there is apparently little competition in the sector and little chance of clients switching firms. Compulsory rotation of audit partners might help to alleviate the comfort-zone problem between auditor and client, but it is a poor substitute for genuine objectivity or competition between firms for clients.

Many investors and regulators have been concerned since 1991 about the import of the Caparo case, which strongly implied that audited accounts were not worth the paper they were written on, because anybody who wasn't a shareholder could not rely on them for investment or lending decisions. The Bannerman Case will not change this situation if auditors are allowed to add explicit disclaimers to their reports to the effect that they cannot be relied upon. How much comfort can a shareholder draw from the accounts if nobody else can rely on them? The strong implication is that if nobody else can rely on them, why should the shareholders?

Following several successful law-suits from the shareholders of collapsed companies, some audit firms have tried to incorporate to become limited liability companies and to move their audit operations off-shore. These further attempts to limit their liability sent very negative signals to financial markets and created an atmosphere of scepticism about the audit process, and there is much work to be done in this area before a sense of security returns.

3. Corporate Governance

This is an area which, like accounting standards, has changed greatly in recent years, but has still not necessarily produced many positive outcomes. Following the introduction of the Combined Code, yet another review of governance is currently taking place (led by Derek Higgs) with the aim of improving the quality of company boardrooms. The key is the appointment of sufficiently able and independent non-executive directors, who can provide an independent check and balance on the company's executive board.

At present, it is felt that there are insufficient numbers of genuinely qualified and independent candidates available and the same faces continually crop up, reducing quality and independence. These non-executive directors are also appointed by, and their remuneration is set by, the very board they are meant to be keeping honest. They often sit on the remuneration committees that set the salaries of the very executive directors that sit on the board.

These inter-relationships and inter-dependencies are not very healthy. Executive directors can choose what they do and don't tell the non-executive directors, further reducing their effectiveness. It is rare for non-executive directors to provide effective checks and balances to the executive directors.

However, the recent troubles and scandals have reduced this pool of talent still further as non-executive directors take the view that the potential personal liabilities they could incur as directors of a collapsed company are too great to be worth the risk. Some insurers have announced that they are withdrawing from the 'directors and officers' liability market, and this factor should not be underestimated in its potential impact on the availability of genuinely independent directors.

The Sarbanes-Oxley legislation recently enacted in the USA calls for a majority of independent directors. It insists that at least some of them have the appropriate skills for their roles and that they, not the executive management, deal with the auditors. However, this will only increase the amount of work and responsibility that non-executive directors undertake. But it is a job that needs to be done and done well.

GLOSSARY

ASB

Accounting Standards Board.

CBI

Confederation of British Industry.

Corporate governance

Rules as to how to conduct the business of running a public company.

Crystallised/realised gains or losses

Accounting gains or losses where there has been a cash impact.

EBITDA

Earnings before interest, taxation, depreciation and amortisation

EPS

Earnings per share (profit after tax divided by the number of ordinary shares in issue).

Equity

Share capital.

FASB

Federal Accounting Standards Board.

FRED

Financial Reporting Exposure Draft.

FRRP

Financial Reporting Review Panel.

FRS

Financial Reporting Standard.

FSA

Financial Services Authority in the UK.

FX

Foreign currency/ foreign exchange.

G4 plus 1

Accounting standard setters in the UK, the USA, Canada, Australia and New Zealand.

GAAP

Generally Accepted Accounting Principals.

IASB

International Accounting Standards Board.

IASC

International Accounting Standards Committee.

ICAEW

Institute of Chartered Accountants in England and Wales.

LSE

London Stock Exchange.

NASDAQ

National Association of Securities Dealers Automated Quotations Index.

NYSE

NY Stock Exchange.

OFT

Office of Fair Trading.

P&L

Profit & Loss statement.

P/E

Price/earnings ratio.

PBIT

Profit before interest and tax.

ROA

Return on assets.

ROCE

Return on capital employed.

ROE

Return on Equity.

SEC

US Securities and Exchange Commission, the stock market regulator for the US.

SSAP

Standard Statement of Accounting Practice.

STRGL

Statement of recognised gains and losses.

The Listing Rules

The rules that listed companies must comply with (the Purple Book).

UITF

Urgent Issues Task Force.

Unrealised gains or losses

Accounting gains or losses where there has yet been no cash impact.

WIP

Work in progress, the stage between raw material and finished goods.

APPENDIX

Financial Reporting Standards in issue

Accounting standards developed by the ASB are contained in 'Financial Reporting Standards' (FRSs). Accounting standards issued by the Accounting Standards Committee are designated 'Statements of Standard Accounting Practice' (SSAPs). Whilst some of the SSAPs have been superseded by FRSs, some remain in force.

See the ASB web-site for full details of all current standards: www.asb.org.uk/technical/standards

FRS 19 - Deferred Tax
FRS 18 - Accounting Policies
FRS 17 - Retirement Benefits
FRS 16 - Current Tax
FRS 15 - Tangible Fixed Assets

FRS 14 - Earnings per Share
FRS 13 - Derivatives and other Financial Instruments: Disclosures
FRS 12 - Provisions, Contingent Liabilities and Contingent Assets
FRS 11 - Impairment of Fixed Assets and Goodwill
FRS 10 - Goodwill and Intangible Assets
FRS 9 - Associates and Joint Ventures
FRS 8 - Related Party Disclosures
FRS 7 - Fair Values in Acquisition Accounting
FRS 6 - Acquisitions and Mergers
FRS 5 - Reporting the Substance of Transactions
FRS 4 - Capital Instruments
FRS 3 - Reporting Financial Performance
FRS 2 - Accounting for Subsidiary Undertakings
FRS 1 (Revised 1996)
- Cash Flow Statements
FRSSE (Effective March 2000)
- Financial Reporting Standard for Smaller Entities

Statements of Standard Accounting Practice (SSAPs)

SSAP 25 - Segmental Reporting
SSAP 24 - Accounting for Pension Costs
SSAP 21 - Accounting for Leases and Hire Purchase Contracts
SSAP 20 - Foreign Currency Translation
SSAP 19 - Accounting for Investment Properties
SSAP 17 - Accounting for Post-balance Sheet Events
SSAP 15 - Status of SSAP 15
SSAP 13 - Accounting for Research and Development
SSAP 12 - Accounting for Depreciation

SSAP 9 - Stocks and Long-term Contracts

SSAP 5 - Accounting for Value Added Tax

SSAP 4 - Accounting for Government Grants

SECURITIES INSTITUTE PUBLISHING

Each publication provides a detailed overview and practical introduction to key topics within financial services.

Our range consists of re–worked and updated notes from our popular courses. These publications are a useful reference for everyone who needs to grasp the basics of a topic – fast!

To place an order or find out more, call now on *020 7645 0680.*

AN INTRODUCTION TO BOND MARKETS

Introduction to Bond Markets provides a comprehensive, authoritative description and analysis of the bond markets. The book considers basic 'plain vanilla' bonds and elementary bond mathematics, before looking at the array of different instruments available. Contents include:

- Bond Yield Measurement
- Corporate Debt Markets
- Eurobonds
- Introduction to Repo
- Risk Management
- Off–Balance Sheet Instruments
- Government Bond Markets
- Emerging Bond Markets.

410pp paperback, ISBN: 1 900520 79 6, 2nd edition

AN INTRODUCTION TO CORPORATE FINANCE
- Transactions and Techniques

Introduction to Corporate Finance provides readers with the key elements of corporate finance. The book introduces the principle techniques used in corporate finance, combined with practical experience and hands-on, numerically orientated case studies.

- Sources of Capital
- Flotations/Initial Public Offerings
- Mergers and Acquisitions
- Management Buy Outs
- Determining the Cost of Capital
- International Equity Offerings
- Valuing Securities

96pp paperback, ISBN: 1 900520 09 5, 1st edition

THE FUNDAMENTALS OF CREST

The Fundamentals of CREST gives a detailed overview of securities administration and settlement through the CREST system. It is illustrated throughout with diagrams and tables, bullet points and summaries.

- Handling Certificated Securities
- Corporate Actions and Claims
- Stock Loans and Collateral.

128pp paperback, ISBN: 1 900520 98 2, 2nd edition

DICTIONARY OF FINANCIAL & SECURITIES TERMS

This updated and greatly expanded 2nd edition gives definitions of frequently used terms in the financial and securities industry. Also included is a comprehensive listing of abbreviations, acronyms and industry websites. Over 2,500 entries.

- What is BIFFEX?
- What does CDP stand for?
- What are the Conduct of Business Rules?
- What is the definition of Debt/Equity Ratio?

Included with the dictionary is a FREE CD–ROM version for users to load onto their PC for easy reference at home or at work.

400pp paperback, ISBN: 1 84307 023 5, 2nd edition

ECONOMIC & MONETARY UNION

Economic and Monetary Union (EMU) is the system that links together the economies and currencies of the participating European countries. The European Central Bank has become responsible for centralised monetary policy. What does the Euro mean for you?

- Convergence
- Impact of the Euro on the markets
- Preparing for the future.

28pp paperback, ISBN: 1 900520 31 1, 1st edition

AN INTRODUCTION TO EQUITY MARKETS

Introduction to Equity Markets provides an overview of the current financial services industry. The book introduces the reader to different types of companies and shares as well as analysis of UK markets. An overview of dealing and settlement in some of the world's major markets is also featured. Contents include:

- Shareholders and Company Law
- Issuing Shares – The Primary Market
- Trading Shares – The Secondary Market
- Settlement of Transactions
- Major Overseas Exchanges and Indices
- Dividends, Bonus Issues and Rights Issues
- Company Accounts.

170pp paperback, ISBN: 1 84307 034 0, 2nd edition

AN INTRODUCTION TO FINANCIAL SPREAD BETTING
- Shares and Indices

Ever wondered what it would be like to live the life of a Millionaire Trader? Anyone, even with the most limited resources, can now open an account with a financial bookmaker and trade just like the 'big boys'. And whilst you may never reach such dizzy heights, the world of financial spread betting can still be an exciting and profitable one. This book will give you all the information you need to know to get you started and guide you to success with a step-by-step approach, uncovering the pitfalls and revealing the secrets of the winning trader.

- Easy To Understand
- Pitfalls To Avoid
- Secrets Of Success
- The Golden Rules Of Financial Spread Betting
- The Psychology Of Trading

144pp paperback, ISBN: 1 84307 069 3, 1st edition

AN INTRODUCTION TO FUND MANAGEMENT

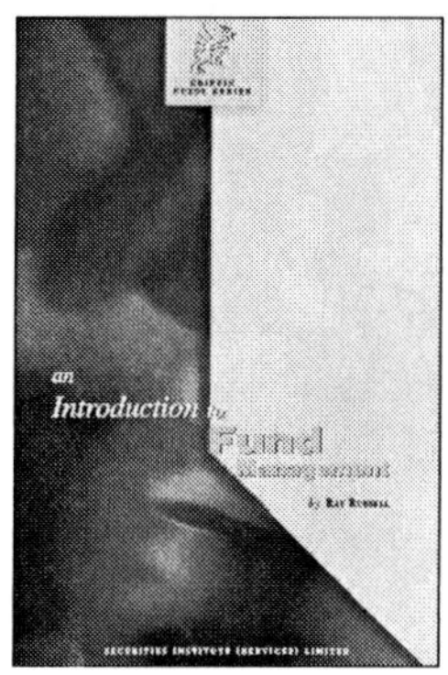

An Introduction to Fund Management introduces readers to the economic rationale for the existence of funds, the different types available, investment strategies and many other related issues from the perspective of the investment manager. Topics include the features and characteristics of funds, portfolio management and administration, performance measurement and investment mathematics. Includes relevant formulae, equations and examples.

- Features and characteristics of funds
- Portfolio management and administration
- Performance measurement
- Investment mathematics.

160pp paperback, ISBN: 1 84307 022 7, 2nd edition

FUNDAMENTALS OF GLOBAL OPERATIONS MANAGEMENT

This book will help you to understand the role of operations terms and what is happening in the industry that impacts on operations. It is ideal for anyone new to or aspiring to become a supervisor or manager.Contents include:

- Operations management
- Markets
- Banking, broking and institutional clients
- Concepts of risk
- Clearing and settlement
- Custody
- Technology
- Regulation and compliance

272pp paperback, ISBN: 1 84307 014 6, 1st edition

AN INTRODUCTION TO THE GILT STRIPS MARKET

Introduction to the Gilt Strips Market provides a thorough description and analysis of gilt strips. The contents describe and define strips as a financial instrument and examine the use and application of gilt strips within the context of the capital markets as a whole. Contents include:

- Zero–coupon bonds
- The yield curve
- Interest rate risk for strips
- Settlement, tax and regulatory issues
- Trading and strategy

192pp paperback, ISBN: 1 84307 006 5, 2nd edition

THE PREVENTION OF MONEY LAUNDERING

This quick guide looks at the scale of the problem and efforts taken to overcome it: an essential reference for all who are concerned to identify attempts at money laundering within their organisation.

- What is money laundering?
- Money laundering and the law
- How do you spot it in the process, and what to do.

48pp paperback, ISBN: 1 84307 005 7, 2nd edition

UNDERSTANDING REGULATION AND COMPLIANCE

Understanding Regulation & Compliance outlines the new regulatory structure in the post-N2 environment, introducing the areas regulated under the *Financial Services and Markets Act 2000*, the role of the *Financial Services Authority* and the rules imposed on firms. It also introduces other important regulatory areas such as *Insider Dealing and Money Laundering*. Topics include:

- Financial Services & Markets Act 2000
- Financial Services Authority
- FSA Handbook
- Control over individuals
- Conduct of business rules
- Client assets
- Improper dealings
- Money laundering

176pp paperback, ISBN: 1 84307 062 6, 3rd edition

INTRODUCTION TO REPO MARKETS

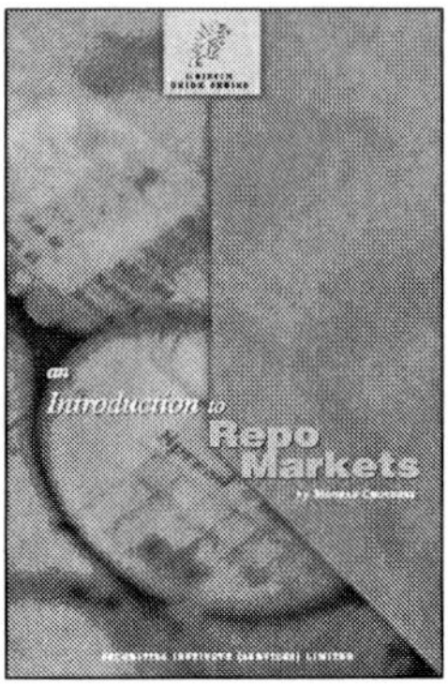

An Introduction to Repo Markets provides a comprehensive description and analysis of the repo markets. The text has been written to cater for those with little or no previous experience of the repo markets, though it also develops the subject matter to sufficient depth to be of use to more experienced practitioners. Contents include:

- Uses and economic functions of repo
- Accounting, Tax and Capital issues
- The UK gilt repo market
- The implied repo rate and basis trading
- Repo and the yield curve

240pp paperback, ISBN: 1 900520 86 9, 2nd edition

AN INTRODUCTION TO SWAPS

An Introduction to Swaps gives a detailed overview of how the various categories of swap work, how they are traded and what they are used for. Topics include interest rate swaps, managing risk, asset swaps, currency swaps. The book is illustrated with over 50 diagrams and tables.

- Managing risk with swaps
- Asset swaps
- Currency swaps.

160pp paperback, ISBN: 1 900520 21 4, 1st edition

Forthcoming titles

Retail Publications

- An Introduction to Derivatives
- Prime Brokerage, Custody and Fund Administration
- Mutual Funds

Securities Institute/Butterworth-Heinemann Global Capital Markets Series

- IPO and Equity Offerings
- Controls, Procedures and Risk
- Clearing, Settlement and Custody
- Managing Technology in the Operations Function
- Relationship and Resource Management in Operations
- Understanding the Markets
- Credit Risk

For further information on this series please call *01865 888180* or visit http://www.bh.com/finance/

We plan to introduce new titles into our retail range in the forthcoming year. All the titles listed are provisional and may be subject to alteration.